JOYSPRICK

AN INTRODUCTION TO THE
LANGUAGE OF JAMES JOYCE

THE LANGUAGE LIBRARY

EDITED BY ERIC PARTRIDGE AND SIMEON POTTER

The Best English	G. H. Vallins
Better English	G. H. Vallins
Caxton and His World	N. F. Blake
Chamber of Horrors	'Vigilans'
Changing English	Simeon Potter
Dictionaries British and American (revised)	J. R. Hulbert
A Dictionary of Sailor's Slang	Wilfred Granville
A Dictionary of Theatrical Terms	Wilfred Granville
Early English	John W. Clark
English Biblical Translation	A. C. Partridge
English Dialects	G. L. Brook
The English Language	Ernest Weekley
Etymology	A. S. C. Ross
Good English: How to Write It	G. H. Vallins
A Grammar of Style	A. E. Darbyshire
A History of the English Language	G. L. Brook
An Introduction to the Scandinavian Languages	M. O'C. Walshe
Jane Austen's English	K. C. Phillipps
The Language of the Book of Common Prayer	Stella Brook
The Language of Dickens	G. L. Brook
The Language of Renaissance Poetry	A. C. Partridge
The Language of Science	T. H. Savory
Modern Linguistics	Simeon Potter
The Pattern of English	G. H. Vallins
The Pitcairnese Language	A. S. C. Ross
Sense and Sense Development	R. A. Waldron
Spelling	G. H. Vallins (revised D. G. Scragg)
Swift's Polite Conversation	Eric Partridge
Tudor to Augustan English	A. C. Partridge
The Words We Use	J. A. Sheard

Anthony Burgess

JOYSPRICK

AN INTRODUCTION TO THE
LANGUAGE OF JAMES JOYCE

ANDRE DEUTSCH

First published 1973 by
André Deutsch Limited
105 Great Russell Street, London WC1

Copyright © 1973 by Anthony Burgess
All rights reserved

Made and printed in Great Britain by
William Clowes & Sons, Limited
London, Beccles and Colchester

ISBN 233 96264 6

TO ERIC PARTRIDGE

Contents

𝔊𝔊𝔊𝔊𝔊𝔊

Phonetic Symbols

꘏꘏꘏꘏꘏꘏

The symbols used (as little as possible) in this book are those of the International Phonetic Alphabet in its narrow form. The following letters carry their usual English values: p, b, m, t, d, n, k, g, f, v, s, z, h, w, r. The other symbols have the values indicated by the italicisations in the key-words that come after:

CONSONANTS

ʃ	*sh*e		θ	*th*in
ʒ	lei*s*ure		ð	*th*en
tʃ	*ch*ew		j	*y*et
ʤ	*Georg*e		l	*l*ife (clear l)
ŋ	si*ng*		ɫ	fi*ll* (dark l)
ɹ	pa*rk* (the retroflex r of American speech)			

VOWELS

iː	s*ee*		ɑː	f*a*ther
ɪ	s*i*t		æ	m*a*n
e	French é as in *blé*		ɒ	h*o*t
eː	caf*é*		ɔː	s*aw*
ɛ	b*e*t		ʊ	p*u*t
ə	bett*er*		uː	bl*ue*
ɜː	w*o*rd		ʌ	b*u*t
ɤ	intermediate between /ʌ/ and /ʊ/ as in Lancashire 'put', 'love'.			

DIPHTHONGS

eɪ	w*ay*		ɔɪ	b*oy*
oʊ	w*oe*		ɪə	h*ere*
aɪ	wh*y*		ɛə	th*ere*
aʊ	n*ow*		ʊə	s*ure*

Preface

🔲🔲🔲🔲🔲🔲

THIS book, such as it is, has been long promised. I have put off writing it chiefly because of my need to earn a living as a novelist (it is still slightly more profitable to write novels than to write about them), and also because of a certain diffidence. These two reasons, or excuses, are cognate. A novelist tends to be out of touch with the world of scholarship (from which one might reasonably expect books on James Joyce's language) and, while the practice of his craft grants him certain insights into the mind of a fellow-novelist, however much more exalted in achievement, it does not predispose him to approach that fellow-novelist's work in the right detached, objective, scientific spirit. There is also the matter of technical equipment, no longer available to the amateur. Language study is an intramural activity, developing rapidly, building up highly specialised disciplines and a terminology that requires a lexicon to itself. I am better qualified to guess at meanings and intentions in Joyce than to analyse his syntax, fish for his deep structures, and taxonomise his tropes.

I had a student in Brunei, the son of a wealthy Malay magnate, who had difficulty in learning what I taught him. He had no difficulty, however, in affording books, and the number of new books he bought at any given time was an index of his learning difficulty. The buying of the books was more sacramental than utilitarian. Whenever, in the last six years, twinges of guilt have pricked me over not starting work on this book of my own, I have bought new books on Joyce written by other men. I have now a very large Joyce library, but I do not know where it is. It has certainly not been with me during the writing of this book. Here in Italy (not even near Trieste), the most unpromising country in the world for Joyce study, I have answered an excruciating signal of accumulated guilt and sat down, with only Joyce's texts by me, to write about the language in those texts. The book that has still to be written about Joyce's language will probably not be written by me, but at least I have learned something of the various ways in which that language may be approached.

The main linguistic work already proceeding on Joyce, inevitably in the United States, is lexicographical. The coinages in *Finnegans Wake* are being separated out according to their exotic origins, and there are already dictionaries of Gaelic and German elements in that polyglot book. There are also computers, including one massive engine in Texas, engaged on word-counts in all Joyce's works, and on concordances between sections of any one work and between one work and another. I have a copy of an earnest-looking book (but since it was produced entirely by cybernetic means perhaps any suggestion of earnestness is out of order) in which I learn how many times Joyce uses the word *the* in *A Portrait of the Artist as a Young Man*. This, I suppose, is a kind of linguistic scholarship. Another, more creative, kind might consist in collating prosodic patterns, making a grammar for Isobel in *Finnegans Wake*, setting out paradigms for sentences in the same book, listing neologisms in *Ulysses*, and so on. But it seems to me that any enquiry into Joyce's use of language must end up in literary criticism, biography, general aesthetics. I find, in this book of my own, that the discussion of a word frequently leads me into its referent, into Joyce's life, into the view of art which Joyce held and incarnated in his novels.

If this book has any value at all, it must be in the attempts it makes to suggest answers to two basic questions which are essentially literary (by which I mean concerned with the aesthetic disposition of language): how does Joyce use language, and why does he use it in that way or those ways? I have concentrated on *Ulysses*, since this is acknowledged to be Joyce's masterpiece, though it is in *Finnegans Wake* that the great difficulties of communication – which linguistic study ought to solve or mitigate – are met. But the fact is that in *Ulysses* there are many kinds of language, while in the *Wake* there is really only one. The elucidation of Porter's or Earwicker's or Joyce's or Finn MacCool's dream must ultimately be in the hands of a kind of philosopher to whom the Joyce lexicographers, biographers and bibliographers send in their reports. But the dream is not intended for total elucidation, since it *is* a dream, and it has been decreed that dreams may only partially be understood.

I think it probable that, on the first centenary of Joyce's death, January 13, 2041, we shall be ready for some such language study of Joyce as, in this Language Library, Professor G. L. Brook has already produced to mark Charles Dickens's centenary. We are too close to Joyce to scrutinise his language historically: as Dr Ellmann has said, we are still trying to become his contemporaries. But, when the time comes, it will be the analytical mind of a Brook (my English Language instructor at Manchester University, where I was a very inept student of the subject) that will be best able to deal with the data embedded in the art, and not a mere novelist like myself. It is one thing to use language; it is quite another to understand how it works.

Bracciano, Rome. September 1971.   A.B.

CHAPTER I

Signs on Paper

𝔊𝔊𝔊𝔊𝔊𝔊

IT was eight o'clock on a June morning with the sun shining on the bay, and the women of Sandycove were at their household chores or doing their shopping, most of them in their customary attire for summer and winter alike of drab wool and, if they were out of doors, a coarse shawl by way of headgear.

Few of them heard and none of them heeded the blasphemous tones of a young plump medical student who appeared on the roof of a tower that rose high above the suburb, and greeted the morning with the Latin words that, in those old pre-vernacular days, began the Roman Catholic mass.

The tower was of the kind called Martello. It had been erected, with many others of its type, all along the coast of Ireland by William Pitt, Prime Minister of England, during the time when an invasion by Napoleon had seemed to be imminent. Now it was rented by the young medical student and his friend for a trifling sum paid annually to the Secretary of State for War. At this time Ireland was still under English rule.

The student, Mulligan, was shaving himself with an old-fashioned cut-throat razor and quipping coarsely at his friend, Stephen Dedalus, who leaned on the top of the stairs that led to the living quarters from the roof and looked coldly at his friend, Mulligan. His friend was shaving with care and oblivious of the cold look.

'Your name, my friend,' he said at length, 'is like a Greek name. Have you ever thought that it was like a Greek name?'

'Yes,' said Dedalus at length. 'It's the name of the first man to be airborne. It was in Crete. The spelling is a little different though, I guess.'

'Is that so?' said Mulligan. 'I thought all your family were Irish but I guess I've not really thought about it all that much before.' He carefully removed a patch of lather and stubble from his chin. 'It's a kind of mockery, I guess. We must go to Athens sometime when I can raise the needful. Haines says there is a little place on the Piraeus where you can get the best ouzo and moussaka in the whole of the Aegean.'

'How long is Haines going to stay here?' said Stephen.

'He's dreadful, isn't he?' said Mulligan after he had shaved further along his plump face. 'He is a heavy Anglo-Saxon who thinks that you're not a gentleman. Jeez, these bloody English. He comes from Oxford and can't understand you, I guess, because you have the Oxford manner.'

'If he stays here,' said Stephen, 'I am off.'

After a time Mulligan inserted a plump hand into the upper pocket of Stephen's black suit and said, 'Lend me your noserag to wipe my razor.' He held it up and said at length: 'It's covered in mucus.'

'Green mucus,' said Stephen. 'Green for Ireland.'

Mulligan moved his plump form to the parapet to look out intently at the bay.

'It's the colour of the sea too, I guess,' he said. 'Look at the sea. When you get near the sea it makes your guts tighten, did you know that? The wine-dark sea is what the Greeks called it. Come and look at it.'

Stephen went over to look at the sea. He leaned coldly on the parapet next to his friend's plump form and looked down at the water. The mailboat was just leaving Kingstown harbour. Neither of them thought that in their lifetimes it would change its name to Dun Laoghaire (pronounced Dunleary), following the withdrawal of English domination from the Irish scene.

'Somebody once called it our mighty mother,' said Mulligan. 'A poet, I guess.'

He turned his large observant eyes from looking at the sea and turned them to look at the face of his friend.

'My aunt thinks you killed your mother,' he said at last. 'She doesn't want us to be, you know, friends.'

'Somebody killed her,' said Stephen. He remembered the time when she was writhing in the agony of terminal carcinoma and all the family were kneeling to pray round her bed. They were a Roman Catholic family, like most of the families of Ireland, but he, Stephen, had recently left the religion of his family and country and was not willing to kneel with the others. He knew that

Mulligan thought he should have knelt down but he just couldn't do it. He wanted to think of himself as liberated. But he knew at the same time that it was very hard to be liberated. He was an Irishman under the domination of the Pope of Rome and the King of England. It would be a long time before liberation.

*

Novelists, like poets, work in the medium of human language, but some may be said to work in it more than others. There is a kind of novelist (conveniently designated as Class 1), usually popular, sometimes wealthy, in whose work language is a zero quantity, transparent, unseductive, the overtones of connotation and ambiguity totally damped. The above* is an attempt at rewriting the opening of Joyce's *Ulysses* in the manner of a Class 1 novelist – one of the American Irvings, say: Stone or Wallace. Such work is closer to film than to poetry, and it invariably films better than it reads. The aim of the Class 1 novel can only properly be fulfilled when the narrated action is transformed into represented action: content being more important than style, the referents ache to be free of their words and to be presented directly as sense-data.

To the other kind of novelist (Class 2) it is important that the opacity of language be exploited, so that ambiguities, puns and centrifugal connotations are to be enjoyed rather than regretted, and whose books, made out of words as much as characters and incidents, lose a great deal when adapted to a visual medium. Drugstore bestsellers, which overwhelmingly belong to Class 1, sometimes nevertheless admit the other category, but only when the lure of the subject-matter – invariably erotic – is stronger than the resistance that the average novel-reader feels towards literary style.

Needless to say, there are stylistic areas where the two classes of fiction overlap. Transparent language – like that of W. Somerset Maugham in his novel *Cakes and Ale* – can be elevated to a high level of aesthetic interest through wit, balance, euphony, and other devices of elegance. Elegance, however, is the most that Class 1 prose can achieve; for dandyism one must go to

* First published in the *New York Times Book Review*. I am grateful to the editor for permission to reprint here.

Class 2 writers. But opaque language can be so self-referring that the reader, legitimately seeking some interest of character and action, may become resentful. A novelist who has brought his reader to the brink of action only to put off the action while he engages in a virtuoso prose cadenza is indulging in the ulti-mate dandyism, which makes the clothes more important than the body beneath. If the promised action is of a violent nature, and the author decides to enjoy a digression on the word itself, finding *violent*, because of its phonic associations with *violet* and *viol*, a somehow unviolent term, then murmurs about artistic irresponsibility will probably be in order. A Class 2 novel, in fact, does not have to be a better work of fiction than a Class 1 novel, but it usually has a better claim to be regarded as literature. The beginning of literary wisdom, at least in the field of the novel, lies in a realisation that Class 1 and Class 2 novelists have some-what different aims. To appreciate James Joyce, one must accept that, for better or for worse, he is irredeemably entrenched in the very heart of Class 2 writing, and that to him literary develop-ment was a matter of digging himself more and more deeply in.

It might be expected that the more extreme Class 2 novelist and the professional linguist should share a common fervour, but there are certain differences between their respective views of the nature of language. To the linguist, the spoken utterance is the primary reality; he wishes to explicate the nature of those meaningful collocations of phonemes, animated by such prosodic features as quantity and accent, which may be loosely termed words, and the structural devices which bind them into larger units of meaning. The Class 2 novelist, on the other hand, seems to take seriously the etymology of the term *literature*, and literally to regard himself as a man of letters: his task is, he believes, to organise visual symbols on the page and, though the reality of sound is obviously important, the form taken by the orthographic signal is hardly less so. Of living novelists, Vladimir Nabokov is a good example of an obsessive to whom the word is both sound and more (or less) than sound. In Humbert Humbert's opening address to the nymphet eponym of *Lolita*, he shows himself aware that her name contains two allophones of the l-phoneme: here he is in the world of the descriptive linguist. But when the appearance of the villain Quilty is foreshadowed in the phrase '*Qu'il t'y mène*', or when, in one of his poems, the author muses on the fact that *diaper* is a palinlogue of *repaid*, then he has passed beyond the territory of linguistics, and even old-fashioned philology, to enter a region of word-magic and word-superstition. In *Pale Fire*, a whole episode of eschatological speculation rests on a typographical error. *Ada* makes great play with anagrams. Nabokov's interest in crossword puzzles (he created the first one in Russian) and games of Scrabble stems from a fascination with words as entities on the printed page. To a literary man the wonder of language lies in its capacity for self-perpetuation through a visual symbology: Latin dies, but Latin remains. The wonder is a legitimate one. Man is naturally *zoon phonoun*, a speaking animal, but to create an alphabet, to transform sound into sight, the instantaneous into the eternal, was to perform a unique miracle. If this wonder is in Nabokov, how much more is it in James Joyce!

In his approach to language, Joyce seems to have set himself up a kind of implied continuum in which, in the middle, groups of letters signify ordinary words but, on the one side, shade into non-linguistic symbols – arithmetical, algebraic, cabbalistic, essentially visual – and, on the other, into attempts at representing inarticulate noise. *Finnegans Wake*, considered, after *Paradise Lost*, the most auditory of all works of literature, cannot well be understood by the ear alone. To take two simple examples: such coinages as 'clapplaud' make auditory sense, but the charmingly simple metathesis 'cropse,' which is a small poem of death and resurrection, has to be seen to be appreciated. *Finnegans Wake* is a representation of a dream, and though much of the dream is conveyed through a mist of disembodied chatter, all in a Dublin accent, not a little of its effect depends on the reader's consciousness of taking in signs on a printed page. Some novels pretend to be after-dinner yarns, but *Finnegans Wake* never pretends to be anything other than a book. The best analogy to it is a musical score, but one of a special and limited kind—a twentieth-century serial work whose structure can only be understood when the eye can pick out the intellectually contrived inversions, retroversions, retroinversions and so on of the atonal *Grundstimmung*.

The range of Joyce's non-auditory semiology is best sampled in the second section of Part II of *Finnegans Wake*. The dreamer Humphrey Chimpden Earwicker, Chapelizod innkeeper, has seen himself fall from a high, if vague, estate, and now his children must take over his place in the world. There are three of them – Kevin, Jerry and Isobel – and the boys, who are twins, contest with each other the right of succeeding to the father, even while they are still in the schoolroom. Part II i represents their tempestuous education, and Joyce hurls straight at us an imaginary textbook full of dream-distorted instruction. This, more than any part of the whole work, totally resists the auditory approach. For, on every page, there are not only ample and confusing footnotes – which seem to be the irrelevant and irreverent comments on learning that the girl Isobel might be expected to make – but also marginal glosses. Jerry, whose chief dream-name is Shem, keeps to the diabolic left with such remarks as *Dont retch meat fat salt lard sinks down (and out)*' – this is a version of the tonic *solfa* scale, incidentally, which has nothing to do with music – while the more earnest Kevin (most frequently met as Shaun) clings to the right with scholarly summaries like 'IMAGINABLE ITINERARY THROUGH THE PARTICULAR UNIVERSAL'. Italic lower and Roman upper case are used as devices of characterisation: obliquity versus loud uprightness. Halfway through the chapter the boys exchange positions and typecases. While Shaun, now on the left, remains pedantic with his '*Catastrophe and Anabasis*' and '*The rotary processus and its reestablishment of reciprocities*', Shem on the right jeers: 'EUCHRE RISK, MERCI BUCKUP, AND MIND WHO YOU'RE PUCKING, FLEBBY.' The boys, who are each half of the great egg who is their father (literally an egg when his first name is changed to Humpty Dumpty), are aware of their inadequacy and are always attempting to merge with each other, thus becoming, together, the man their father was. But they succeed only in borrowing – as symbolised in the typography – characteristics of each other.

One footnote contains, among other symbols, the following: ⊓, Δ, Λ, ⊏. These can be understood only if we have followed Joyce's preoccupation with the initials of the names of his hero and heroine. Humphrey Chimpden Earwicker is frequently met, in dream-actuality or dream-memory, as HCE,* and these initials are sewn into the fabric of the prose like a monogram (HCE – his

* This is a musical phrase, but only in Germany, where H stands for B natural. (It is the key in which Wagner's *Tristan and Isolde* ends.) Joyce does not appear to exploit the musical connotation.

dream). They are often filled out anew to some such characteristic phrase as 'Here Comes Everybody' (Earwicker is universal man), 'Haveth Childers Everywhere' (father of us all), 'Human Conger Eel' (he is vital, devious, slippery and may be thought of as an animated penis), or, as in the very opening of the book, 'Howth Castle and Environs' (he is not only a builder of cities, he is a city himself). They are sometimes hidden inside a word, such as the misspelling 'HeCitEncy' (and here we may note that the forged letters with which the Irish journalist Piggot sought to ruin Parnell – an avatar of HCE – provide a totally visual *leitmotiv* for *Finnegans Wake*: Piggot incriminated himself by misspelling *hesitancy* as *hesitency*, and Joyce's own misspellings are a convenient symbol for the betrayal of a leader, as well as a reminder that HCE has a speech hesitation which emanates from sexual guilt). The initials are occasionally rearranged to make a genuine vocable like 'hec' or 'ech' or even 'Hecech'. Auditory recognition of the holy sign is not always easy and not always intended, but when Joyce takes the one initial E and plays symbolic tricks with it, then the eye must work alone and the ear shut down. The E falls on its back, and then Earwicker – more like a beetle than the insect his name suggests – is helpless, his legs kicking in the air, dishonoured, dead: Ш. The E is, as in the footnote we are engaged on, made to fall forward, so that its prongs grip the ground, and Earwicker has been converted into a great ancient monument like Stonehenge, with a powerful association of fertility ceremonies: Ⅲ. In other words, he is a man when his E is upright, but either a dead insect or a deathless god when the letter loses its human balance.

Earwicker's wife is named Ann, but she is identified in his dream with the river Liffey and given the title Anna Livia Plurabelle. (The *Plurabelle* indicates her beauty and plurality: she contains all rivers and all women.) The initials ALP are subjected to the same kind of play as HCE. 'A Laughable Party' is the pseudonym she uses to sign one of her messages; she is triply celebrated in some Latin the boys are learning: '*Apis amat aram. Luna legit librum. Pulla petit pascua.*' As an acronym, her initials convey her natural majesty and beauty. An ALP may be represented as a triangle, and an equilateral triangle is a delta. *Delta* suggests richness through its very apt denotation of a triangular alluvial (the word is hidden in her full name) tract at the mouth of a river, but the very look of the letter – Δ – is, in inversion, that of the pubic mane. When the twins engage on their geometry lesson (ALP is our 'geomater', or earth-mother), they discover that all mathematical or scientific enquiry is nothing more than curiosity about what lies under our mothers' skirts.

Now we know what E and Δ stand for, we may not find it too difficult to guess at the meanings of E and Λ. The two signs evidently symbolise the two brothers. HCE is a builder of cities, but ALP is nature, ultimate creation, the dynamic river which the artist must tap. For Shem the artist (a James like Joyce; indeed, Joyce is one of his identities), the creative mother must mean more than the authoritarian father, but his creativity, in comparison with hers, is maimed, incomplete, lacking in a bottom or fundament. Hence the delta without a base: Λ. Shaun, who aspires to political leadership, the building and ruling of communities, is closer to HCE than to ALP, but he lacks his father's dynamism, itself an aspect of sexual energy. Hence his sign – Ɛ: an E that has no penis.

Joyce made much of the mathematical content of *Finnegans Wake* and considered, too hopefully, that it was this element that might make the book appeal to scientists. But his mathematics is really arithmology – number as magical symbol. In Part II i he draws heavily on the Cabala. The All-Father is 1 and his consort is 0 – 'Ainsoph, this upright one, with that noughty besighed him zeroine'. Introduce the dart to the egg, or the phallus to the Elizabethan 'thing of nought', and we have 10, symbol of creation. The chapter ends with a recital of the Cabalistic numbers which represent the various stages by which creation moves to completion: 'aun do tri car cush shay shockt ockt ni geg.' 'Cush' (5) can also be 'kish' (we move from the back of the mouth to the front for the vowel) – a point of division appropriate to the two brothers. If Shaun-Kish is Christ, Shem-Cush must be Antichrist: the latter's enmity is symbolised in the footnotes by a sketch of a thumbed nose and spread fingers (the traditional 'long bacon' gesture), with the legend 'Kish is for anticheirst, and the free of my hand to him!'

Number is important everywhere in *Finnegans Wake*: indeed, it is the only element in the long dream which is not subject to deformation and dissolution. In true dreams we can take three slices of cake from a plate containing ten and leave five or four or none, but Joyce's arithmetic is solid and unnonsensical (this may be taken, among other things, as a tribute to the mathematician Lewis Carroll, inventor of the prototype of Joyce's superjabberwocky and a stutterer and lover of little girls, like HCE). The supporting characters of the dream are identified by number more than by name – the twelve men who can be a jury, the apostles, the months of the year; the four men who can be the evangelists or the provinces of Ireland or the posts of the Earwicker bed; the twenty-eight girls of St Bride's Academy who are the days of the month of Joyce's birthday, sometimes augmented to twenty-nine by Isobel, the 'leapyear girl': when not bissextile, they can be divided by four and turn into a rainbow. The narrative is periodically punctured by a clap of thunder which, whatever its lexical or onomatopoeic makeup, is always – for nine of its appearances – composed of exactly one hundred letters. Its tenth and last rumbling is marked by a slight difference: one letter has been added. This makes the total number of thunderletters in the book one thousand and one, reminding us that a single Irish night contains as much legend and beguilement as all those Arabian ones. When ALP converts the shattered body of her dead lord HCE into gifts for her children, the gifts are presented in all their mad particularity, and there are exactly one hundred and eleven – 111, symbol of plenitude, the limbs of HCE when he has become an ancient fertility monument.

The very year in which the events of the dream take place is a symbolic number – 1132 – which has no real historical significance. 32 stands for man's fall and 11 for his resurrection. The continuation of life is really the resumption of a cycle: when we have counted up to 10 on our fingers we must start all over again with 11, emblem of resumption. 32 feet per second per second, as Mr Bloom in *Ulysses* reminds himself without fully understanding it, is the acceleration rate of all falling bodies, including those of Adam, Parnell, Satan and Humpty Dumpty. 32 is also a traditional arithmological symbol for Christ, since he was thirty-two years old when he died and rose again. All this numerological play, childish though it may seem, is a firm device for holding down the centrifugal whirl of myth and language which is *Finnegans Wake*.

In both this work and *Ulysses*, Joyce evidently sees as a valid literary technique the forcing of words – whether as phonemic or orthographic structures – into a semiotic function which shall be iconic more than conventional. Words must not only stand for their referents: they must mimic them as well, even at the risk of their own disintegration. When the demagogic Shaun exalts himself into a kind of vulgar Christ, guzzling a glutinous last supper, he eats steak, peas and bacon which, as they are chewed, turn into 'kates and eaps and naboc'; the boiled protestants (or potatoes: during the Irish famine Protestant evangelists made converts through the bribe of potato soup) and cabbage which accompany them are munched into (x for consonant; o for vowel) 'xoxxoxo and xooxox xxoxoxxoxxx': there seems to be a dash of meat extract there as well. This is, of course, a wholly visual device, but one wonders if some of the seeming onomatopoeia of *Ulysses* is not also addressed primarily to the eye. Mr Bloom's cat cries 'Mkgnao!', then 'Mrkgnao!' and then, at her intensest, 'Mrkrgnao!' Given milk, she runs to lap it with a 'Gurrhr!' S. J. Perelman, in one of his humorous essays, describes a cat that goes 'Mrkgnao!' but adds that it had obviously read *Ulysses*. It seems sometimes that Joyce uses letter-combinations to suggest the presence of a noise through the absence of lexical sense, rather than to convey its sonic quality through onomatopoeic means.

The 'Sirens' episode of *Ulysses* begins with a catalogue of disjunct phrases and vocables, ending:

> Last rose Castille of summer left bloom I feel so sad alone.
> Pwee! Little wind piped wee.
> True men. Lid Ker Cow De and Doll. Ay, ay. Like you men.
>   Will lift your tschink with tschunk.
> Fff! Oo!
> Where bronze from anear? Where gold from afar? Where hoofs?
> Rrrpr. Kraa. Kraandl.
> Then, not till then. My eppripffftaph. Be pfrwritt.
> Done.
> Begin!

We discover, when we are past this prelude and into the narrative, that we have been presented with the verbal equivalent of musical themes, all of which have to be developed in Joyce's complex *fuga per canonem*. The musical form is appropriate, since the art of music must preside over a chapter whose Homeric counterpart is Odysseus's encounter with the Sirens, but there can be little doubt that Joyce welcomes the excuse to deform words for the sake of mystification, to puzzle the reader with strange signs on the page. He attempts to do with words what the musician does with notes, producing, for instance, a tremolo: 'Her wavyavy-eavyheavyeavyeevyey hair uncomb:'d', a set of staccato chords: 'I. Want. You.', hollow fifths: 'Blmstdp' (the vowels of 'Bloom stood up' are omitted on the analogy of suppressed thirds in common chords):

The musical significance of these tricks is minimal: it is the eye more than the ear that is intrigued.

But of Joyce's genuine auditory success in the exploitation of iconic tropes there can be little doubt. Stephen's ashplant has its own voice, its ferrule 'squealing at his heels' as he walks: 'My familiar, after me, calling Steeeeeeeeeeephen.' In Glasnevin cemetery, Mr Bloom muses on ways of keeping the dead in mind:

Besides how could you remember everybody? Eyes, walk, voice. Well, the voice, yes: gramophone. Have a gramophone in every grave or keep it in the house. After dinner on a Sunday. Put on poor old greatgrandfather Kraahraark! Hellohellohelloamawfullyglad kraark awfullygladaseeragain hellohello amarawf kopthsth. Remind you of the voice like the photograph reminds you of the face.

But immediately after this brilliant mimesis we have to take 'Rtststr!' as 'a rattle of pebbles'.

It is in the 'Circe' episode of *Ulysses*, where magic dissolves time and space and evil sorcery turns men into swine, that language tends to become mere noise or – the visual equivalent of noise – a mess of letters. A 'deafmute idiot with goggle eyes . . . shaken in Saint Vitus' dance' dribbles 'Grhahute!' and 'Ghagha-hest.' Bells of cyclists cry 'Haltyaltyaltyall.' A gong says 'Bang Bang Bla Bak Blud Bugg Bloo.' The quoits of the bed on which Bloom's wife has committed adultery go 'Jigjag. Jigajiga. Jigjag.' The bells of St George's church toll 'Heigho! Heigho!' Kisses warble 'Leo!' and twitter 'Icky licky micky sticky for

Leo!' Baby Boardman hiccups 'Hajahaja.' Davy Byrne yawns
'Iiiiiiiiiaaaaaaaach!' The fire brigade goes 'Pflaap!' A gramophone,
echoing that earlier one of Bloom's musing, rasps 'Whorusalam-
inyourhighhohhhh . . .' The eight beatitudes growl incoher-
ently 'Beer beef battledog buybull businum barnum buggerum
bishop.' A gasjet wails 'Pooah! Pfuiiiiii!' A waterfall cascades
'Poulaphouca Poulaphouca Poulaphouca Poulaphouca'. A nanny-
goat bleats 'Megegaggegg! Nanaannanny!' 'The dummy of
Bloom, rolled in a mummy' goes 'Bbbbblllllbbblblodschbg?'
A button snaps 'Bip!' Bella's 'sowcunt barks' 'Fohracht!'
Black Liz, the hen clucks 'Gara. Klook. Klook. Klook.' Shakespeare, of all people, growls 'Weda seca whokilla farst.' Lynch,
pommelling on the brothel sofa, goes 'Rmm Rmm Rmm
Rrrrrrmmmmm.' The croppy boy, giving up the ghost, chokes
'Horhot ho hray ho rhother's hest.' While the Voice of all the
Blessed cries 'Alleluia, for the Lord God Omnipotent reigneth',
the Voice of all the Damned must palinlogise the laudation to
'Htengier Tnetopinmo Dog Drol eht rof, Aiulella!' A retriever,
picking up Major Tweedy's 'Salute!', barks 'Ute ute ute ute ute
ute ute ute.'

Joyce's pleasure in the fracting of language and the notation
of noise is an aspect of his fascination with what seems to him to
be the magic of the whole semiological process. He considers
the act of signalling rather more important than the message it
attempts to convey. Through various kinds of signs, auditory
as well as visual, parts of the world try to make contact with other
parts – animal, vegetable and mineral, men and gasjets, dogs and
pianolas, bowels and the heavenly host. It is possible to see his
non-linguistic signals as elements in a Malinowskian interpretation of man's need to communicate. Semiology to Joyce is
phatic – a means of making social contact – and those peripheral
or totally extra-linguistic signs which, more than any other author,
he revels in, are legitimate modes of communication.

Joyce was in advance of the communications pundits of our
own day in recognising the fascination of media in themselves
(like Marshall McLuhan) and the width of the whole field of
semiology (like Roland Barthes). In *The Mechanical Bride* McLuhan
says:

The French symbolists, followed by James Joyce in *Ulysses*, saw that
there was a new art form of universal scope present in the technical

layout of the modern newspaper. Here is a major instance of how a
by-product of industrial imagination, a genuine agency of contem-
porary folk-lore, led to radical artistic developments. To the alerted
eye, the front page of a newspaper is a superficial chaos which can lead
the mind to attend to cosmic harmonies of a very high order. Yet when
these harmonies are more sharply stylized by a Picasso or a Joyce, they
seem to give offence to the very people who should appreciate them
most.

This probably means that Joyce saw the virtues of the visual, as
well as the auditory, shock. In a small way, the practice of es-
chewing hyphens and, for that matter, inverted commas was, and
still is, a means of forcing the eye into a new look at language.
That undammed river of Molly Bloom's closing monologue, in
which there is not even minimal punctuation, is essentially a
visual effect, since to read the monologue aloud inevitably en-
tails introducing breathing-spells and a variety of speech-tunes:
whether he wishes to or not, the ear-reader is forced into pro-
viding punctuation. The imposition on the 'AEolus' chapter of
Ulysses of a history of the newspaper headline is justified by the
symbolism (god of the wind – editor – journalism – rhetoric,
etc.), but the true motivation has to do with a relish for the newspaper medium itself, its power to shock a reader into attention.
The manner in which, on any page of a newspaper, we move
from subject to subject without logical progression, finds a
counterpart in the interior monologue, where the mind dips into
its own private newspaper and comes up with topics at random.
If the newspaper layout influenced Joyce, so did newer communication media. He was the first man to open a cinema in Dublin
(the failed Volta), and the rapid shifting of images in 'Circe'
owes as much to cinematic technique as to Joyce's reading of Flaubert's *La Tentation de Saint Antoine*. It ought to be remembered
that Joyce was far from averse to the filming of *Ulysses* and even
suggested that George Arliss (whom he had seen enact Disraeli)
should be cast as Bloom. Radio and television both have a large
part to play in the action of *Finnegans Wake*. It could be argued
plausibly that this interest in the media had something to do
with Joyce's Jesuit background.

Henceforth our concern must be with Joyce the manipulator
of ordinary human language, in which his best magic is performed, and not just as an eccentric comic who is over fond of the

humorous possibilities of noise and gibberish, or a conjuring trickster who, finding mystification and surprise to be a source of innocent power over his audience, must be indulged as a Christmas uncle is indulged. Joyce may stretch language inordinately both in lexis and prosodic organisation, but he can point to great prototypes – Rabelais, Sterne, Swift, Milton, Shakespeare himself. His magic is mostly genuine, like theirs, inducing the kind of wonder and joy one feels in the presence of natural sublimity.

CHAPTER 2

The Dublin Sound

🎵🎵🎵🎵🎵🎵

In *A Portrait of the Artist as a Young Man*, the undergraduate
Stephen Dedalus engages in a conversation on aesthetics with
the Dean of Studies, an English Jesuit, 'humble follower in the
wake of clamorous conversions' (was Joyce, incidentally, already
thinking of the title and subject-matter of his last book?). The
Dean leads the conversation towards the 'useful arts' and, talking
of the art of filling a lamp with oil, uses the term 'funnel', which
Stephen has not met in that context: his word is 'tundish',
which the Dean does not know at all. (Like many dialect terms
in Anglo-Irish, it is of respectable Middle English ancestry.)
Stephen feels 'a smart of dejection that the man to whom he was
speaking was a countryman of Ben Jonson', and says to himself:
'The language in which we are speaking is his before it is mine.'
This is sentimental and self-pitying, not easily forgivable even
in an undergraduate, and to erect a sense of alienation on a single
pair of words is perhaps going too far.

From a lexical point of view there are hardly any differences
between Stephen's English and that of the Dean of Studies.
Stephen, like the characters in Swift's *Polite Conversations*, will
ask for tea or washing water to be 'filled out'; he will eat a
crubeen (a pig's or sheep's foot) and, in Cork, a drisheen or black
pudding. He will refer to oxters rather than armpits and know that
'plain' in Buck Mulligan's 'Ballad of Joking Jesus' means beer
(*locus classicus* in Flann O'Brien's *At Swim-Two-Birds*: 'Do you
know what it is I am going to tell you? A pint of plain is your
only man.') But we need no special dictionary to read Joyce's
plainer works. If, in *Finnegans Wake*, the Gaelic element is large,
this is because Gaelic is a foreign language with a special claim
on Joyce's attention, since ancient Ireland coexists in the book
with various kinds of modern Ireland, but the Gaelic lexicon
that has already been compiled out of *Finnegans Wake* is no

bigger than the German one. The Italian one (which has probably already been completed) must be the biggest of all. The works of William Faulkner and J. D. Salinger are foreign compared with *Ulysses*: Stephen and the Dean of Studies meet on everything but funnels and tundishes.

But the continuation of Stephen's dejected musing brings us to the real point about Anglo-Irish linguistic differences:

... How different are the words *home, Christ, ale, master* on his lips and on mine! I cannot speak or write these words without unrest of spirit. His language, so familiar and so foreign, will always be for me an acquired speech. I have not made or accepted its words. My voice holds them at bay. My soul frets in the shadow of his language.

An American Joyce scholar recently saw in those four words 'powerful symbols of dispossession', but one may reasonably ask what dispossession has to do with ale. What make Stephen's soul fret are the simple differences between his own pronunciation of the words and that of the Dean of Studies. He feels the inferiority of a provincial in the presence of a metropolitan or ruling-class accent: his case is little different from that of a Lancastrian or Northumbrian in the days when public-school English had power to frighten and humble. But Stephen feels the weight of three kinds of authority in the Dean's speech – the ruling class, the Imperial power, the international Church. His own accent is not merely provincial, it is also that of a subject people.

Let us consider the sounds they use respectively in these four key-words. The Dean has a diphthong in *home* – /oʊ/ or /əʊ/, while Stephen has a long open vowel – /ɔː/. The diphthong of Stephen's *Christ* approaches /ʌɪ/ while the Dean's is a patrician /aɪ/. Stephen has, for *ale*, a high tense vowel followed by a clear l – /eːl/ – while the Dean has a diphthong with a dark l – /eɪɫ/. The Dean's *master* has a back vowel and a final schwa – /mɑːstə/; Stephen's has a front vowel and ends with a retroflex r – /mæstɹ/. Stephen, or Joyce, has cunningly chosen words that demonstrate very well the main phonic differences between the speech-systems of the English and Irish capitals.

Ironically, it is Stephen's own inherited Dublin speech that is nearer to the tongue of Ben Jonson than the Dean's Received Pronunciation (RP). Those admirers of Joyce who place him close

to Shakespeare are unassailable in one respect: the English on
which Joyce was reared, and out of which he contrived a literature even more idiosyncratic than Shakespeare's, had and still
has many of the phonetic features of the language of Elizabethan
London. What are thought of as essentially Anglo-Irish versions
of the vowel in *tea*, *sea* and *beat* and the diphthong in *my*, *eye*,
fight are close enough to the regular usages of Shakespeare.
Falstaff puns on *reasons* and *raisins*; as late as Alexander Pope *line*
is a rhyme for *join*. To be accurate about Dublin English, one
must say that it fossilises most of the features of Pope's English,
eighteenth-century English, and that this English still had many
of the features of Elizabethan English. Joyce has to meet Swift
and Sterne and Addison before he meets Shakespeare.

This is probably not the place to discuss the Great Vowel
Shift which helped to turn the English of Henry V into that of
our own day. It is enough to say that, in the mediaeval period of
English, the *i* of *shine* had the value it still has in the Romance
languages – /iː/ – and the *ou* of *mouse* (a spelling introduced by the
Normans to replace the more reasonable Anglo-Saxon *mūs*)
meant what it still means to the French – /uː/. These vowels,
being long, became increasingly unsteady (the tongue, like any
other muscular organ, does not like to hold the same rigid position for too long a time), and they wavered themselves into the
state of diphthongs. *Shine*, in RP, now has a firm /aɪ/, while
mouse has a solid /aʊ/. But for a lengthy period both diphthongs,
while their second element recalled quite clearly the parent vowel,
though now in a shorter and slacker form, kept the first element
in a vague central region. Shakespeare probably said /ʃəɪn/ and
/məʊs/. A diphthong with a first element further back in the
mouth than /ə/ was also acceptable – something like /ʌɪ/ or
/ʏɪ/ for *shine* and /ʌʊ/ or /ʏʊ/ for *mouse* – and these, which we
associate with Queen Anne and Swift and the *Spectator*, are still
to be heard in Japanese and German Dublin.

When words like *shine* and *eye* and *I* and *my* jumped out of that
/iː/ slot which is the front upper region of the mouth, words
containing a double e – *meet*, *beet*, *queen* and so on – forgot that
their vowel was a Continental /eː/ whose length was symbolised
in the orthographic doubling, and rose to fill the high gap, giving
the pronunciation in /iː/ that we share with the Elizabethans and
the Augustans. On the rung below the ee-words were the ea-

words – *meat, beat, quean* (meaning prostitute) and the rest. The second element of the digraph had been a signal to make a low e – /ɛː/, but now the low e became a high one, filling the empty slot. Words like *lady* and *make*, which in Chaucer's time had a Continental a – as in *chatte* or *acqua* – now rose to take over the discarded /ɛː/. This general rising has continued, front and back, so that *meat* and *beat* have risen to the limit, giving us awkward homophones (the awkwardness is spectacularly to be observed in *queen* and *quean*, but the latter has dropped out of general use). *Make* rose to become /me.k/ and was then diphthongised into /meɪk/. The modern Dublin situation has resisted those awkward homophones but has accepted, for the most part, the placing of words like *name* and *cream* in the same vocalic slot. The whole story of changing English pronunciation is a long one. The above partial summary is merely meant to show that the demotic speech of Dublin, and other parts of Ireland, has remained close to the standards which were accepted as cultivated and aristocratic in the days of the great Dean of St Patrick's.

At its lower social levels, the English of Joyce's town continues to resist the influence of British RP and to combine with eighteenth-century English vowels and diphthongs consonants that show the influence of Erse. The Irish thetatismus which levels /θ/ and /ð/ under the dental /t/ and /d/ respectively (not alveolar, as in RP), the combination /tr/ in which the first element is so dentalised as to lead some writers of Irish comedy to represent it as *thr* (as in *thrue* for *true*), the tendency to make affricates of medial and final /t/ and /d/ – these seem to derive from consonantal usage in the native Celtic tongue, as does the clear l which is found in all positions, in opposition to the RP darkening of l in final positions and before other consonants (RP *well* = /wɛl/; RP *built* = /bɪlt/). Educated Anglo-Irish speech retains the clear l but follows RP usage in respect of the other consonants, except that – as in all varieties of Irish English as well as American English and many British dialects – the letter r, in whatever position, is taken as a phonemic signal and not as a mere ghost or vowel-length sign. While speakers of RP pronounce *park* and *warm* as /pɑːk/ and /wɔːm/ respectively, most Irishmen join Americans in pronouncing the written r as a retroflex consonant, or enunciating the preceding vowel with the tongue in a retroflex position.

Educated Irish speakers of English show willingness to come close to RP vocalic usage, though they are not always happy about the close diphthongs /eɪ/ and /oʊ/. We can be fairly sure, when reading *Ulysses*, that Joyce intends Mulligan to hail 'our great sweet mother' as /ðə siː/ and not /də seː/, though, when he refers to the time when 'the French were on the sea', he has in mind the popular song 'The Shan Van Vocht' –

> The French are on the sea,
> Says the Shan Van Vocht . . .
> They'll be here without delay,
> And the Orange will decay . . .

– and presumably adjusts his pronunciation accordingly. How Stephen Dedalus, in this phase of his postgraduate career, is meant to pronounce English we cannot be sure. Mulligan refers to Stephen's 'Oxford manner', which seems to imply an adjustment of his native phonemes to educated British usage, but we cannot easily accept that Stephen is now pronouncing *home* as /hoʊm/ or /hʏʊm/ or /həʊm/ and *master* as /mɑːstə/. To level *ee* and *ea* under the one vowel /iː/, to pronounce *might* as /maɪt/ and *join* as /dʒɔɪn/, while retaining other native vocalic and diphthongal usages, is the most an Irishman need do to qualify as an 'educated' speaker.

Ulysses, which is a conspectus of so many things, may be taken as implying the whole spectrum of Dublin speech, and it would be amusing to sketch out a cline, with the speech of drabs and jarveys near the bottom and that of characters like J. J. O'Molloy and Professor MacHugh somewhere at the top. As it is, for the most part, far more enlightening to hear *Ulysses* read aloud (with the score on one's knee) than to peruse it silently, it is useful for the teacher of a Joyce course to have a rough repertory actor's notion of accent differentials. In the 'Cyclops' chapter, where the narrative is entrusted to an anonymous low Dubliner, the idiom provides a clue to the accent:

I was just passing the time of day with old Troy of the D.H.P. at the corner of Arbour Hill there and be damned but a bloody sweep came along and he near drove his gear into my eye. I turned around to let him have the weight of my tongue when who should I see dodging along Stony Batter only Joe Hynes.

Here 'just' and 'bloody' and 'tongue' will probably have the vowel /ʊ/, whereas a more educated speaker would prefer, if not /ʌ/ (the RP vowel), at least /ɤ/. 'My eye' will be /mɪj ʌɪ/, 'around' something like /əˈræʊnd/, 'Stony Batter' probably /stɔːnɪ bætˢr./, the /t/ palatalised and affricated. The *ing* of 'passing' and 'dodging' will be pronounced as a syllabic /n/. Compare this with the way in which we may imagine Professor MacHugh, in the 'AEolus' episode, enunciating the following:

– What was their civilisation? Vast, I allow: but vile. Cloacae: sewers. The Jews in the wilderness and on the mountaintop said: *It is meet to be here. Let us build an altar to Jehovah.* The Roman, like the Englishman who follows in his footsteps, brought to every new shore on which he set his foot (on our shore he never set it) only his cloacal obsession. He gazed about him in his toga and he said: *It is meet to be here. Let us construct a watercloset.*

The *wh* of 'what' will be pronounced as an unvoiced semivowel /ʍ/, whereas educated British usage would prefer /w/. The *a* of 'civilisation' could be, instead of the RP /eɪ/, the vowel /eː/ or even one approaching /ɛː/. 'Vast' would not be RP /vɑːst/ but Elizabethan /væ.st/, but 'vile' would conform with British usage except for the clear l (/vaɪl/, not /vaɪɫ/). The r in 'sewers', 'wilderness', 'here', 'altar' and 'shore' would be pronounced as a weak retroflex consonant. The o-letter in 'Jehovah', 'Roman' and 'toga' should be interpreted not as a diphthong (RP /oʊ/) but as the open sound /ɔː/.

It is intriguing to consider how Leopold Bloom's speech would fit into the spectrum. His idiom, either in dialogue or interior monologue, is lacking in the broader Dublin features: it approaches the emancipated or 'Londonised' language we associate with, say, Ignatius Gallaher the journalist (a character in the *Dubliners* story 'A Little Cloud' who, in *Ulysses*, has become a newsman's myth). We may imagine Bloom – the 'cultured allroundman' as Lenehan, in a moment of rare Dublin generosity, calls him – as possessing the ability to vary his speech according to the company, but as being totally incapable of sinking to the lowest demotic Dublinese. Certain actors playing the part of Bloom in radio adaptations of Ulysses, before the advent of the stage *Bloomsday* and the film *Ulysses*, both of which established Milo O'Shea as an authoritative interpreter of the role, attempted to give a 'Jewish' quality to Bloom's speech. Whatever 'Jewish' means, it can have no significance in terms of voice or accent. Jews using English as a second language may bring to it the usages of Yiddish or Ladino, but Bloom, though his father was Hungarian (and, according to the 'Circe' episode, capable of English like 'One night they bring you home drunk as dog after spend your good money'), is clearly a product of lower middle-class Dublin and its language is his. Stage 'Jewishness' of the adenoidal variety would be totally out of place. We may take Bloom as a mediator, in speech as in other things, between his earthy wife Molly and the poetic Stephen.

Few readers have any doubts about the phonetic content of, say, Molly's final words:

... and I thought well as well him as another and then I asked him with my eyes to ask again yes and then he asked me would I yes to say yes my mountain flower and first I put my arms around him yes and drew him down to me so he could feel my breasts all perfume yes and his heart was going like mad and yes I said yes I will Yes.

Joyce has established on her very first appearance that she has no education. 'It must have fell down,' she says, and 'Tell us in plain words'. But the implied lower-class Dublin speech does not fit in well with her declared background. Her father was a major in the Gibraltar garrison and her mother was Spanish. (I spent three years as a soldier in Gibraltar and find both her father's rank and his marriage implausible, but let that pass.) Molly would grow up speaking Andalusian Spanish (Joyce makes her approach it as through a Hugo grammar) and a kind of pseudo-patrician English imposed by her father's position in a closed and highly snobbish garrison society. Coming to Dublin as a young woman she would be unlikely to relinquish a sort of ruling-class accent and idiom. I think we have to remember that Joyce's shaping of his heroine's mind and speech owed more to the reality of his wife's perpetual presence than to the fictional imagination. Consider the following:

Well I feel very knocked up to day you don't know what a thunder-storm is but if you went through one here you would not be worth much it was something dreadful it began last night about half past nine we were in the dining room with a few people and as it had been raining all day the people did not expect it and all of a sudden it came on lightening thunderbolts I thought it was our last I was almost stiff with fright for about twenty minutes then it poured and we went to bed about half past ten but I did not sleep then a hurricane began and lightening which lasted till halfpast five this morning . . .

That is not a discarded draft for 'Penelope' but a letter from Nora Joyce.

It is no exaggeration to state that Joyce takes, among all the varieties of spoken English, only that of his own town seriously. When British English is heard in *Ulysses*, it is always in the form of a music-hall parody. In the 'Cyclops' chapter 'the stern pro-vostmarshal, lieutenantcolonel Tomkin-Maxwell ffrenchmullan Tomlinson' murmurs to himself 'in a faltering undertone': 'God blimey if she aint a clinker, that there bleeding tart. Blimey it makes me kind of bleeding cry, straight it does, when I sees her cause I thinks of my old mashtub what's waiting for me down Limehouse way.' In 'Circe' the author Philip Beaufoy, on whose story 'Matcham's Masterstroke' Bloom has innocently wiped his morning fundament, attacks this 'particularly loathsome conduct' thus:

You funny ass, you! You're too beastly awfully weird for words! I don't think you need over excessively discommodate yourself in that regard . . . We are considerably out of pocket over this bally pressman johnny, this jackdaw of Rheims, who has not even been to a university . . . You ought to be ducked in the horsepond, you rotter!

American English is represented by a spirited parody of an evangelistic exhortation:

Elijah is coming washed in the Blood of the Lamb. Come on, you winefizzling ginsizzling booseguzzling existences! Come on, you doggone, bullnecked, bettlebrowed, hogjowled, peanutbrained, weaseleyed fourflushers, false alarms and excess baggage. Come on, you triple extract of infamy! Alexander J. Christ Dowie, that's yanked to glory most half this planet from 'Frisco Beach to Vladivostok. The Deity ain't no nickel dime bumshow. I put it to you that he's on the square and a corking fine business proposition. He's the grandest thing yet and don't you forget it. Shout salvation in king Jesus. You'll need to rise precious early, you sinner there, if you want to diddle the Almighty God. Pflaaaap! Not half. He's got a coughmixture with a punch in it for you, my friend, in his backpocket. Just you try it on.

Dublin English is apotheosised, in *Finnegans Wake*, to a universal language capable of absorbing all others. It is a remarkable prosodic achievement in that it can move from the lowest street colloquial to the sesquipedalian pedantic without transitional devices:

He addle liddle phifie Annie ugged the little craythur. Wither hayre in honds tuck up your part inher. Oftwhile balbulous, mithre ahead, with goodly trowel in grasp and ivoroiled overalls which he habitacularly fondseed, like Haroun Childeric Eggeberth he would caligulate by multiplicables the alltitude and malltitude until he seesaw by neatlight of the liquor wheretwin 'twas born, his roundhead staple of other days to rise in undress maisonry upstanded (joygrantit!), a waalworth of a skyerscape of most eyeful hoyth entowerly, erigenating from next to nothing and celescalating the himals and all, hierarchitectitiptitoploftical, with a burning bush abob off its baubletop and with larrons o'toolers clittering up and tombles a' buckets clottering down.

But, of course, the seeds of this mad variety are already present in the real speech of Dublin, with its ability to encompass obscenity, seedy scraps of half-remembered learning, malapropism, the grandiloquent structures of oratory, euphony and balance for their own sake regardless of meaning. To take such a vehicle of social communication seriously is essentially not to take it seriously, since it has ludic elements in it which disappeared from British English when the Puritans came. There is nothing more preposterous than the sound of *Finnegans Wake* when professors read passages from it aloud in American or (far, far worse) British English. The book is based on the sound of Dublin English and it encompasses its entire orchestral spectrum. We may read the opening in the style of George Bernard Shaw –

riverrun, past Eve and Adam's, from swerve of shore to bend of bay, brings us by a commodius vicus of recirculation back to Howth Castle and Environs

– and the ending in the style of any lachrymose old biddy in the snug –

Bussoftlhee, mememormee! Till thousendsthee. Lps. The keys to. Given! A way a lone a last a loved a long the

– but, as the last word governs the first, we are in the same sentence and hence speaking with the same voice.

CHAPTER 3

Dialect and Idiolect

🔒🔒🔒🔒🔒🔒

IF we wish to regard *Ulysses* as a kind of compendium of Dublin speech, it is important to be able to distinguish between what belongs to the common stockpot and what is the idiosyncratic property of that character or this. To affirm, because we find it in the book, that 'Shite and onions' was in 1904 a popular Dublin interjection is to do an injustice to Mr Simon Dedalaus's inventive powers. To tap the general flow we must go to the minor characters – particularly the anonymous 'collector of bad and doubtful debts' who narrates the story of Bloom's encounter with the Cyclops. The anonymity is essential to the Homeric symbolism (Odysseus gave his name as 'Noman'), and it imposes a kind of featurelessness on the language – lively and picturesque enough, but unindividual and uninventive:

So we turned into Barney Kiernan's and there sure enough was the citizen up in the corner having a great confab with himself and that bloody mangy mongrel, Garryowen, and he waiting for what the sky would drop in the way of drink.

Demotic Irish speech has solved to its own satisfaction all the problems of constructing long sentences:

And one night I went in with a fellow into one of their musical evenings, song and dance about she could get up on a truss of hay she could my Maureen Lay, and there was a fellow with a Ballyhooly blue ribbon badge spiffing out of him in Irish and a lot of colleen bawns going about with temperance beverages and selling medals and oranges and lemonade and a few old dry buns, gob, flahoolagh entertainment, don't be talking.

Subordinate clauses are rarer than in British English; phrases and clauses may be freely coordinated:

Then he starts hauling and mauling and talking to him in Irish and the old towser growling, letting on to answer, like a duet in the opera.

And the two shawls killed with the laughing, picking his pockets the bloody fool and he spilling the porter all over the bed and the two shawls screeching laughing at one another.

Even when subordination is used, there must be no subordinating conjunction if it can be avoided:

The bloody mongrel let a grouse out of him would give you the creeps.

One of the bottlenosed fraternity it was went by the name of James Wought alias Saphiro alias Spark and Spiro, put an ad in the papers saying he'd give a passage to Canada for twenty bob.

So J.J. puts in a word doing the toff about one story was good till you heard another . . .

Native Celtic usage sometimes appears in the treatment of a verb: '. . . an orangeman Blackburn does have on the registration . . .' (As also here in Master Patrick Aloysius Dignam's interior monologue in the 'Wandering Rocks' episode: 'One of them mots that do be in the packets of fags Stoer smokes that his old fellow welted hell out of him for one time he found out.') The Irish flavour of the narration can be carried merely by the typical inversion of subject and invariable verb-form *says*:

– Are you a strict t.t.? says Joe.
– Not taking anything between drinks, says I.
– What about paying our respects to our friend? says Joe.
– Who? says I. Sure, he's in John of God's off his head, man.
– Drinking his own stuff? says Joe.
– Ay, says I. Whisky and water on the brain.

'Itself' has an emphatic function not known in British English:

Let us drink our pints in peace. Gob, we won't be let even do that much itself.
Mean bloody scut. Stand us a drink itself.

A locative is sometimes used instead of, or as a reinforcement for, a possessive adjective:

. . . and the face on him all pockmarks would hold a shower of rain. Bloom was talking and talking with John Wyse and he quite excited with his dunducketymudcoloured mug on him and his old plumeyes rolling about.

There is a fair range of expletives – 'Arrah', 'by Jesus', 'Good

Christ!', 'Christ McKeown', 'Gob', 'Begob', 'O Jakers',
'Bloody wars' and so on – and a great deal of slang that is as
much British as Anglo-Irish, though much of it would be
regarded as old fashioned in the England of 1904.

I'm hanging on to his taw now for the past fortnight and I can't get
a penny out of him.
That the lay you're on now?
There he is in his gloryhole.
The old one was always thumping her craw.
. . . by the holy farmer, he never cried crack till he brought him home
as drunk as a boiled owl . . .
He's not as green as he's cabbagelooking.
– Could you make a hole in another pint?
– Could a swim duck? says I.
That explains the milk in the cocoanut and the absence of hair on the
animal's chest.
Playing cards, hobnobbing with flash toffs with a swank glass in their
eye, drinking fizz and he half smothered in writs and garnishee orders.

All the above, which I have pulled out of the text at random, have
an early nineteenth-century flavour about them, and only one is
specifically Anglo-Irish: 'by the holy farmer' – a euphemism for
by the Holy Father.

What gives this whole representative piece of Dublinese an
undeniable charm is its gossipy flow. The narrator likes nobody
in Dublin, except the treater of the moment, but he knows
everybody and has an intense interest, however malicious, in
their doings. Like Mr and Mrs Breen, for instance:

Cruelty to animals so it is to let that bloody povertystricken Breen out
on grass with his beard out tripping him, bringing down the rain.
And she with her nose cockahoop after she married him because a
cousin of his old fellow's was pew opener to the pope. Picture of him
on the wall with his smashall sweeney's moustaches. The signor Brini
from Summerhill, the eyetallyano, papal zouave to the Holy Father,
has left the quay and gone to Moss street. And who was he, tell us? A
nobody, two pair back and passages, at seven shillings a week, and he
covered with all kinds of breastplates bidding defiance to the world.

There is solidity here, the exactly called-up image of malice, and
the enthusiasm of the dislike breeds a kind of oratory, even
though it often has to depend on ignorance and dim memories
of stage melodrama: 'all kinds of breastplates bidding defiance

to the world.' The Dubliner of Joyce's youth, however low, was the citizen of a small community in which everybody knew everybody else, ensuring that there should be no lack of bitchy subject-matter for gossip; his town was litigious, music-loving, afire with loud politics, and full of Church Latin. At its coarsest, Dublin speech could have a smell of culture about it:

Someone that has nothing better to do ought to write a letter *pro bono publico* to the papers about the muzzling order for a dog the like of that. Growling and grousing and his eye all bloodshot from the drouth is in it and the hydrophobia dropping out of his jaws.

Despite the powerful impression that Molly Bloom gives us of possessing a language all her own (or all Nora Joyce's), in reality her final monologue is in a very generalised idiom and may be taken as the female counterpart, linguistically speaking, of the 'Cyclops' narrator's:

I was a bit wild after when I blew out the old bag the biscuits were in from Benady Bros and exploded it Lord what a bang all the woodcocks and pigeons screaming coming back the same way that we went over middle hill round by the old guardhouse and the jews burial place pretending to read out the Hebrew on them

This is in order since, to match Bloom's 'Noman', she is All-woman: her inner speech must be the great turgid sea from which all life arises, not a bright idiosyncratic piece of flotsam like Mrs Breen's 'O don't be talking. He's a caution to rattlesnakes . . . He has me heartscalded.'

The most memorable of all the *Ulysses* idiolects is that of Mr Dedalus, whose speech is exactly modelled on that of Joyce's own father. In *A Portrait* his saltier utterances are suppressed and we hear mainly a shabby-genteel jauntiness: '. . . there's a crack of the whip left in me yet, Stephen, old chap. We're not dead yet, sonny. No, by the Lord Jesus (God forgive me) not half dead.' There is no dilution of his essential richness in *Ulysses*:

Was that Mulligan cad with him? His *fidus Achates*? . . . Down with his aunt Sally, I suppose, the Goulding faction, the drunken little costdrawer and Crissie, papa's little lump of dung, the wise child that knows her own father . . . He's in with a lowdown crowd. That Mulligan is a contaminated bloody doubledyed ruffian by all accounts. His name stinks all over Dublin. But with the help of God and His blessed mother I'll make it my business to write a letter one of these days to his mother or his aunt or whatever she is that will open her eyes as wide as a gate. I'll tickle his catastrophe, believe you me . . . I won't have her bastard of a nephew ruin my son. A counterjumper's son. Selling tapes in my cousin Peter Paul McSwiney's. Not likely.

'Noisy selfwilled man,' thinks Mr Bloom, looking at him. 'Full of his son.' But Mr Dedalus can be eloquent about anything, like the bad rhetoric Ned Lambert reads to him in 'AEolus':

Agonising Christ, wouldn't it give you a heartburn on your arse?

This is his view of his daughters:

Wait awhile. You're like the rest of them, are you? An insolent pack of little bitches since your poor mother died. But wait awhile. You'll all get a short shrift and a long day from me. Low blackguardism! I'm going to get rid of you. Wouldn't care if I was stretched out stiff. He's dead. The man upstairs is dead.

The character of the man comes out clearly in the collocation of coarse violence, remembered bits of school learning, a certain dramatic gift, pathetic snobbishness, selfishness. Among what may be termed second-rank characters in *Ulysses*, only "the bloody doubledyed ruffian' Buck Mulligan approaches him for idiolectal interest.

Mulligan (who may be taken as a touched-up photograph of Oliver St John Gogarty in his youth) has the task of giving *Ulysses* a liturgical start. This can only be done blasphemously:

For this, O dearly beloved, is the genuine Christine: body and soul and blood and ouns. Slow music, please. Shut your eyes, gents. One moment. A little trouble about those white corpuscles. Silence, all.

These few lines are enough to tell us that Mulligan enjoys blasphemy and is a medical student with literary tastes. In a sense he is a completion of Mr Dedalus, who began as a medical student without finishing the course, has not reached the stage of liking blasphemy for its own sake, only for its expletive value, and also has a literary background. If Mr Dedalus can say '*fidus Achates*', Mulligan can quote the Greeks: '*Epi oinopa ponton . . . Thalatta!* *Thalatta!*' He knows Swinburne – 'Isn't the sea what Algy calls it: a grey sweet mother?' – but immediately after can refer to the sea as 'snotgreen'. He is wittily eloquent, as when he reminds

Stephen of 'the night in the Camden hall when the daughters of Erin had to lift their skirts to step over you as you lay in your mulberrycoloured, multicoloured, multitudinous vomit'. He says little that does not have a sexual or scatological reference. Of Bloom he says to Stephen: 'The wandering jew. Did you see his eye? He looked upon you to lust after you. I fear thee, ancient mariner. O, Kinch, thou art in peril. Get thee a breechpad.' He is essentially a malicious clown with an education, and his final appearance, in which he mocks at the apparition of Stephen's dead mother, is appropriately 'in particoloured jester's dress of puce and yellow and clown's cap with curling bell':

BUCK MULLIGAN (*shakes his curling capbell*): The mockery of it! Kinch killed her dogsbody bitchbody. She kicked the bucket. Our great sweet mother! *Epi oinopa ponton.*

Lenehan, who first appears in the *Dubliners* story 'Two Gallants', is characterised there as a small sports writer and a willing jester to anyone with money. Like Mr Dedalus, he carries round the orts of an education – 'That takes the solitary, unique, and, if I may so call it, *recherché* biscuit' – but he totally lacks force of character. In the 'AEolus' episode of *Ulysses*, Joyce makes him exemplify many of the silly minor rhetorical tropes which are imposed by the symbolism: 'Madam, I'm Adam. And Able was I ere I saw Elba . . . Clamn dever . . . Muchibus thankibus . . . We will sternly refuse to partake of strong waters, will we not? Yes, we will not. By no manner of means,' and so on. Among the small men of the book – Tom Rochford, McCoy, Ned Lambert, Father Cowley, Ben Dollard and the many more – he alone is idiolectally memorable, but only because of the silly clownishness.

The professional and semi-professional men – J. J. O'Molloy, O'Madden Burke, Professor MacHugh and, to some extent, the editor Myles Crawford – tend to merge in the reader's memory. This is because we first, and sometimes finally, meet them in the 'AEolus' episode, when, unlike Lenehan, they are giving examples of the higher kinds of rhetoric. They speak like books. Here is Professor MacHugh again (his title is a courtesy one bestowed by his cronies; he is a teacher of Latin):

The Greek! *Kyrios!* Shining word! The vowels the Semite and the Saxon know not! *Kyrie!* The radiance of the intellect. I ought to profess Greek, the language of the mind. *Kyrie eleison!* The closetmaker and the cloacamaker will never be lords of our spirit. We are liege subjects of the catholic chivalry of Europe that foundered at Trafalgar and of the empire of the spirit, not an *imperium*, that went under with the Athenian fleets at Ægospotami. Yes, yes. They went under. Pyrrhus, misled by an oracle, made a last attempt to retrieve the fortunes of Greece. Loyal to a lost cause.

(Lenehan's response to this is to mock-weep: 'Boohoo! Owing to a brick received in the latter half of the matinée. Poor, poor, poor Pyrrhus!') Myles Crawford is earthier than his legal and classical friends and, like Mr Dedalus, is capable of shafts of irritable invective: 'All balls! Bulldosing the public! Give them something with a bite in it. Put us all into it, damn its soul. Father Son and Holy Ghost and Jakes McCarthy.' He tells Bloom to tell Keyes: 'He can kiss my royal Irish arse. Any time he likes, tell him.'

Most lovers of Joyce's pre-*Wake* work will reluctantly admit that the bulk of the supporting cast of Dubliners in *Ulysses* have not recovered from the paralysis they are suffering from in the short stories where they first appear. Martin Cunningham has the honour of appearing in *Finnegans Wake* as well as in *Dubliners* and *Ulysses*, but he is never established as a firm creation – in the way that even the smallest personage of a Dickens novel bristles with life. We remember J. J. O'Molloy for his epigram 'Sufficient unto the day is the newspaper thereof' and little Boody Dedalus for saying 'Our father who art not in heaven' and Corny Kelleher for his tag 'Do you follow me', but the general effect of the *Ulysses* background, in so far as it is manifested in the way people speak, is strangely unvital. But perhaps not strangely. Our interest in Bloom should, no doubt, be sharpened by our lack of interest in most of his fellow-Dubliners. Bloom's Antinous, Blazes Boylan, is a mere shadow – a small-town dandy with a flower-stalk in his teeth, saying things like 'That'll do, game ball' and 'May I say a word to your telephone, missy?' – but it is in Bloom's thoughts and Molly's broodings after the adulterous event and, more than anywhere, in the mythopoetic phantasmagoria of the 'Circe' chapter that he is elevated to a disruptive engine. Nighttown is the place where the dull Dubliners are given real life and real character and, in the process, lose their regular real-life idiolects.

Bloom himself seems, when he is presented to us directly, a character with no very distinctive mode of speech. (The interior monologues carry the true memorable pungency, as we shall see.)

But, in the narrative of 'Cyclops', he is made into a kind of sea-lawyer with his 'You see, he, Dignam, I mean, didn't serve any notice of the assignment on the company at the time and nominally under the act the mortgagee can't recover on the policy'. He is argumentative and full of big words like 'phenomenon'. It is in the reports and memories of others that he talks learnedly and, as Lenehan puts it, has a touch of the artist. In the 'Eumaeus' episode, where Bloom and Stephen have a late-night colloquy in the cabmen's shelter, the prose-style is that of a cliché-ridden newspaper article and it imposes on Bloom not only an unnatural stupidity but a way of speaking rather like a police statement 'gorblimeyed' by the desk sergeant:

– It beats me, Mr Bloom confided to Stephen, medically I am speaking, how a wretched creature like that from the Lock Hospital, reeking with disease, can be barefaced enough to solicit or how any man in his sober senses, if he values his health in the least. Unfortunate creature! Of course, I suppose some man is ultimately responsible for her condition. Still no matter what the cause is from . . .

In the 'Circe' scene the style of Bloom's interior monologues is externalised into his spoken statements – though here it is not easy to say what is spoken and what is merely imagined. There is a great deal of dramatised wish-fulfilment, so that Bloom as mayor, emperor, whipping-boy or Ruby Pride of the Ring has to borrow a mode of speech and a vocabulary appropriate to each fleeting role. If, in real life, we met Mr Micawber in a dark room, we would know it was Mr Micawber from his peculiar tropes; Bloom in similar circumstances we would not know. Only if we were granted the power to enter the minds of fictional characters, in some literary man's heaven where they had become as real as the blessed saints, would we know we were savouring essential Bloom. Indeed, it is difficult to imagine any of Dickens's characters as possessing minds as opposed to pieces of simple psychological clockwork: Bloom has little other than that endless inner flow.

Stephen Dedalus is the only one of Joyce's characters whom we know from early childhood to a kind of maturity, and we have to approach his spoken language diachronically. It is noteworthy that, in *A Portrait*, he says little until he has reached the undergraduate stage: the talk is mostly left to his parents, teachers and

Joysprick

schoolmates. But, when he has achieved the state of free flight, he is almost unnaturally eloquent. The long aesthetic disquisition he forces on Lynch is an animated essay which we are persuaded only by Lynch's down-to-earth interruptions to accept as speech. His declaration of intent to Cranley, just before the book ends, is stagy – like something from Joyce's very stagy drama *Exiles*:

> I will tell you what I will do and what I will not do. I will not serve that in which I no longer believe, whether it call itself my home, my fatherland, or my church: and I will try to express myself in some mode of life or art as freely as I can and as wholly as I can, using for my defence the only arms I allow myself to use – silence, exile, and cunning.

In *Ulysses* we must, as we must with Bloom, listen to the interior monologues to find out the essential Stephen that lies under the brittle erudite exterior. Our main meetings with Stephen, after the early-morning scene when he talks tiredly but cleverly and yet also humanly (he is reasonable, for instance, about drinking tea with lemon since the milkwoman has not yet arrived), are in very exceptional circumstances. In *A Portrait* he gave a long lecture to Lynch on aesthetics; in *Ulysses* he gives a long lecture on Shakespeare to Eglinton, Best and Lyster in the National Library. In the lying-in hospital we meet him through the distorting lenses of parodies (or properly pastiches) of English prose-styles from Malory to Carlyle; thus we do not really hear his voice at all. In the brothel district he is drunk and inconsequential and is also set upon by magic, so that he becomes a comic cardinal and a Montmartre flesh-tout. In 'Eumaeus' he is sober but tired and a little sharp. In 'Ithaca' it is all abstract catechism and reported speech. Stephen is always just a little too good, or clever, to be true. He puts on an act and is thus closer to the legal and classical men of 'AEolus' than he might be supposed to be willing to admit.

He is, though clever and far too well-read, willing enough to engage the actualities of Dublin life, and streets and names are as much in his conversation (rightly so, since he is someday to write *Ulysses*) as great poetic lines and chunks of tortuous theology. The story he calls *A Pisgah Sight of Palestine or the Parable of the Plums* is far too fluently delivered, but it is about real Dubliners:

> – Two Dublin vestals, Stephen said, elderly and pious, have lived

fifty and fiftythree years in Fumbally's lane ... They want to see the
views of Dublin from the top of Nelson's pillar. They save up three
and tenpence in a red tin letterbox moneybox. They shake out the
threepenny bits and a sixpence and coax out the pennies with the blade
of a knife. Two and three in silver and one and seven in coppers. They
put on their bonnets and best clothes and take their umbrellas for fear
it may come on to rain.

This chronicle of low life, pointless but with every low-life point
noted, is really intended as a rebuke to the high-flying oratory-
lovers he has been forced to listen to: it is intended to counter the
big words and lofty abstractions. One would like to know whether
he has told the story before, rehearsed it, written it down. For
all its colloquial verve it sounds like something carefully composed
on paper and learned by heart.

There are two further points to be made about the speaking
Stephen. One is that the learning with which he dazzles his
listeners is sometimes very superficial and secondhand. Professor
MacHugh tells him of Antisthenes the sophist, who 'wrote a
book in which he took away the palm of beauty from Argive
Helen and handed it to poor Penelope'. Stephen's interior monologue flashes: 'Poor Penelope. Penelope Rich.' This is a link
with the Shakespeare discourse that is to come, in which he will
calmly palm off Professor MacHugh's gobbet of learning as his
own. The other point is that he is capable of tenderness, which his
father is not. The brief scene in 'The Wandering Rocks', where
he meets his sister Dilly, is touching. But the deeper emotions
are never expressed in words; they lie in the tortured mind of the
young poet:

She is drowning. Agenbite. Save her. Agenbite. All against us. She
will drown me with her, eyes and hair. Lank coils of seaweed hair
around me, my heart, my soul. Salt green death.
   We.
   Agenbite of inwit. Inwit's agenbite.
   Misery! Misery!

The feeling, though it requires poetic diction and a memory of
obscure Middle English homiletic writing, is genuine enough.
   Standards and terms appropriate for ordinary books – in this
context *Ulysses* may be regarded as an ordinary book – do not
work well when brought to a discussion of *Finnegans Wake*.

Nevertheless, this must be regarded as a novel, and not as an obscure mystical codex: it has characters and things happen, or seem to happen, in it. There is speech, and its tones are of anonymous Dublin:

O tell me all about Anna Livia! I want to hear all about Anna Livia. Well, you know Anna Livia? Yes, of course, we all know Anna Livia. Tell me all. Tell me now. You'll die when you hear. Well, you know, when the old cheb went futt and did what you know. Yes I, know, go on. Wash quit and don't be dabbling. Tuck up your sleeves and loosen your talktapes. And don't butt me – hike! – when you bend. Or whatever it was they threed to make out he thried to two in the Fiendish park. He's an awful old reppe. Look at the shirt of him! Look at the dirt of it! He has all my water black on me.

This is clear enough to show us that it is dialogue between two washerwomen who could well live in the same street as the narrator of the 'Cyclops' chapter. Idiolect is a different matter. Anna Livia herself is so fluid a character that she cannot be identified – as a Dickens character is identified – by a sentence or so of speech, but her daughter Isobel is always radiantly recognisable:

... Now open, pet, your lips, pepette, like I used my sweet parted lipsabuss with Dan Holohan of facetious memory taught me after the flannel dance, with the proof of love, up Smock Alley the first night he smelled pouder and I coloured beneath my fan, pipetta mia, when you learned me the linguo to melt.

Her idiolect owes something to Swift's 'little language' and her trademark endearment is either 'ppt' or some allomorph of it – like the 'pepette' and 'pipetta' here – which comes straight from the *Journal to Stella*. Kate the cleaning-woman in Earwicker's pub has generally a grumbling manner of speech: '... who bruk the dandleass and who seen the blackcullen jam for Tomorrha's pickneck I hope it'll pour.' The twelve customers who so frequently change their names and occupations – we meet them first as 'the doorboy, the cleaner, the sojer, the crook, the squeezer, the lounger, the curman, the tourabout, the mussroomsniffer, the bleakablue tramp, the funpowtherplother, the christymansboxer' – are fond of words ending in *-ation*, and this is a means of recognising them:

... are the porters of the passions in virtue of retroratiocination and, contributing their conflingent controversies of differentiation, unify their voxes in a vote of vaticination, who crunch the crusts of comfort due to depredation, drain the mead for misery to incur intoxication, condone every evil by practical justification and condam any good to its own gratification ...

Earwicker himself is most easily identifiable by a mechanical trick. He manifests his guilt in a stammer:

– Amtsadam, sir, to you! Eternest cittas, heil! Here we are again! I am bubub brought up under a camel act of dynasties long out of print, the first of Shitric Shilkanbeard (or it it Owllaugh MacAuscullpth the Thord?), but, in pontofacts massimust, I am known throughout the world wherever my good Allenglisches Angleslachsen is spoken by Sall and Will from Augustanus to Ergastulus, as this is, whether in Farnum's rath or Condra's ridge or the meadows of Dalkin or Monkish tunshep, by saints and sinners alike as a cleanliving man and, as a matter of fict, by my halfwife, I think how our public at large appreciates it most highly from me that I am as cleanliving as could be and that my game was a fair average since I perpetually kept my ouija ouija wicket up. On my verawife I never was nor can afford to be guilty of crim crig con of malfeasance trespass against parson with the person of a youthful gigirl frifrif friend chirped Apples ...

The two sons, Shem and Shaun, are more easily recognised through personal manner than through modes of speech. Shaun as a boy is humourless and plodding in the schoolroom, vindictive and cruel in play, while Shem tends to an alternation of irreverence and gloom, even self-pity. Shaun turns into a demagogue skilled at empty blustering, sentimental cajoling (especially when his audience is a female one), and plausible maxim-making:

Never back a woman you defend, never get quit of a friend on whom you depend, never make face to a foe till he's rife and never get stuck to another man's pfife. Amen; ptah! His hungry will be done! On the continent as in Eironesia. But believe me in my simplicity I am awfully good, I believe, so I am, at the root of me, praised by right cheek Discipline! ... Down with the Saozon ruze! ... Like the regular redshank I am. Impregnable as the mule himself.

Like Buck Mulligan, he enjoys blasphemy but – being inside a dream – he is able to take it to the limit, ending in a self-identification with Jesus Christ. The mature Shem, who has opted for 'carberry banishment' (exile), 'mum's for maxim' (silence), and 'handy antics' (cunning), is more selfeffacing, humbler, but not much more likeable.

CHAPTER 4

Interior Monologue

𝔊𝔊𝔊𝔊𝔊𝔊

ONE of the problems Joyce set himself in writing *Ulysses* was that of reconciling more than epic length with the strictures of dramatic form. He wished to expand in the Homeric manner but to contract like Sophocles – to encompass a great deal of human adventure and to set it all on a single summer's day in Dublin. The obvious solution was to make a more detailed examination of his characters' acts and thoughts than had been considered necessary by traditional fiction. Bloom must not only eat and drink but defecate and masturbate; he must also uncover his thoughts and feelings and velleities. Molly Bloom must meditate more exactly on her lovers than Emma Bovary had been permitted to do. But the existing techniques for expressing thought and feeling were insufficient. Hence the 'stream of consciousness' or 'interior monologue' – an endless commentary from the main characters on the data thrown at them by life, always unspoken, sometimes chaotic, following subterranean laws of association rather than logic. The device had been used before – by Dickens, Samuel Butler, even Jane Austen – but never on the scale or to the limits employed by Joyce. After all, he lived in the psycho-analytic era, though he considered he had nothing to learn from either Freud or Jung.

Joyce's immediate forebear in the use of the stream of consciousness technique was the Frenchman Dujardin, who had employed consistently though somewhat lightheartedly a kind of inner telegraphese (unspoken Mr Jingle) for the hero's thoughts in his novel *Les Lauriers sont Coupés*. Joyce saw the possibilities of the device to a far greater degree than Dujardin, but at the same time was aware of dangers undreamt of by that somewhat dilettante novelist. For to present, in total realism and devastating nakedness, the whole flood of a character's inner life was not properly to create art: it was merely to record as one of the new clinicians might record. What was needed was some kind of directional monitor. The flow had to be shaped and enclosed, and one means of doing this was suggested by the ultimate aim of the whole book, which was to find Homeric parallels in every one of the pedestrian adventures of a Dublin advertisement broker. Leopold Bloom is a modern Ulysses, so he has to encounter Sirens and a Cyclops, visit the island of Circe, be rebuffed by the god of the winds, and so on. Each adventure suggests a special literary technique and a special presiding symbol. Moreover, an art or science and an organ of the human body must be celebrated in each section, so that the totality appears as both an image of a culture and (as in Swedenborg) the figure of a man. If Bloom is in the land of AEolus, it is in order to restrict his monologue to journalism and to fill it with references to wind:

Funny the way those newspaper men veer about when they get wind of a new opening. Weathercocks. Hot and cold in the same breath. Wouldn't know which to believe. One story good till you hear the next. Go for one another baldheaded in the papers and then all blows over.

Similarly, in 'The Lotus Eaters', with its strong floral-herbal motif, even his re-reading of a love letter from Martha Clifford is showered in petals:

He tore the flower gravely from its pinhold smelt its almost no smell and placed it in his heart pocket. Language of flowers. They like it because no-one can hear. Or a poison banquet to strike him down. Then, walking slowly forward, he read the letter again, murmuring here and there a word. Angry tulips with you darling manflower punish your cactus if you don't please poor forgetmenot how I long violets to dear roses when we soon anemone meet all naughty nightstalk wife Martha's perfume.

In 'AEolus', rhetoric and lungs preside, preventing Bloom from brooding on food, sex or the internal combustion engine. In 'The Lotus Eaters', the botanic and phallic hold him in a mild narcissistic rhythm and lead him to a bath and contemplation of 'the dark tangled curls of his bush floating, floating hair of the stream around the limp father of thousands, a languid floating flower'.

The tone and rhythm of Bloom's interior monologue are highly distinctive. There is an unadorned matter-of-factness about the statements he makes to himself which is appropriate to his honesty – a quality he shares with few of his fellow-Dubliners. He is not a man of much education, but he is shrewd and, knowing the world well like his classical counterpart, he is contentedly disillusioned. Within the limits which life has set him, and which he philosophically accepts, he knows what he wants. For breakfast, for instance:

Ham and eggs, no. No good eggs with this drouth. Want pure fresh water. Thursday: not a good day either for a mutton kidney at Buckley's. Fried with butter, a shake of pepper. Better a pork kidney at Dlugacz's. While the kettle is boiling.

Reading, we are convinced that this is how thoughts flow through the mind, and we forget that most of our inner life, especially when it is concerned with elemental matters like bodily wants, is preverbal. Desiring ham and eggs for breakfast, we experience sensations of appetite, memories of the mixed taste of salt, albumen and fat, and perhaps even erect a brief image of the frying pan with the food sizzling in it. But we do not say to ourselves: 'Ham and eggs, yes.' Joyce is working in a verbal medium and has to contrive a verbal equivalent for the preverbal flow.

Joyce's refusal to separate, by some device of punctuation or relineation, the récit from the monologue led early readers of *Ulysses* to complain. Fifty years after first publication, few would have difficulty in distinguishing between the inner Bloom and the outer world in the following:

He crossed to the bright side, avoiding the loose cellarflap of number seventyfive. The sun was nearing the steeple of George's church. Be a warm day I fancy. Specially in these black clothes feel it more. Black conducts, reflects (refracts is it?), the heat. But I couldn't go in that light suit. Make a picnic of it. His eyelids sank quietly often as he walked in happy warmth. Boland's breadvan delivering with trays our daily but she prefers yesterday's loaves turnovers crisp crowns hot.

And there is a virtue in keeping the two on, as it were, the same sonic level. We have always accepted the convention that words can, in an ordinary narrative, stand for things or events; juxtapose closely this revolutionary convention, which makes words stand for the stream of consciousness, and it becomes acceptable by association. Moreover, it is not really possible to separate the observed from the observer. Still, we have to be told that Bloom crossed the street, for he would be unlikely to say to himself: 'Cross street now to bright side. Must avoid loose cellar-flap of number seventyfive' (though this kind of implausibility is common enough in *Les Lauriers sont Coupés*). His muscles would be in charge, or an unthinking heliotropism, and the mind would not really be engaged. It is doubtful also whether his monologue could encompass the statement 'The sun was nearing the steeple of George's church.' The visual observation would not register as the knowledge that the day is too warm for a funeral suit registers. Bloom has a twentieth-century man's interest in popular science, and in the thought that heat does something to black we reach a genuinely verbal level. (Normally when Bloom thinks about words – or about scientific laws, for that matter, such as the one about falling bodies – he thinks about them desultorily, with a small sort of curiosity that does not ask to be satisfied. Humming the Commendatore's recitative from *Don Giovanni*, he wonders whether perhaps *teco* means *tonight*, but he does not add: 'Must find out. Italian dictionary in National Library perhaps.') When his eyelids sink 'quietly' it is the author who is with us, not his hero, since Bloom cannot be made to say: 'Eyelids sinking quietly often. Happy warmth.' That 'happy' is a pinprick of a word. A post-Flaubertian author is not, it seems, effacing himself as much as he should: he is making a general statement about one of his characters. But the word is easily acceptable as denoting the most elementary state of physical wellbeing, not the condition of Bloom's mind. The final sentence conjoins author's statement and character's observation. We see Bloom's eyelids, then we see the breadvan, then we are inside Bloom's head seeing the breadvan.

The phrases which make up Bloom's thought-paragraphs are very short and usually very sure of themselves: there is sometimes the danger of Joyce's turning them into epigrams. In the 'Laestrygonians' chapter Bloom is absorbed with thoughts of food (it is the lunch-hour; Homeric cannibals preside):

Sardines on the shelves. Almost taste them by looking. Sandwich? Ham and his descendants mustered and bred there. Potted meats. What is home without Plumtree's potted meat? Incomplete. What a stupid ad! Under the obituary notices they stuck it. All up a plumtree. Dignam's potted meat. Cannibals would with lemon and rice. White missionary too salty. Like pickled pork. Expect the chief consumes the parts of honour. Ought to be tough from exercise. His wives in a row to watch the effect.... With it an abode of bliss. Lord knows what concoction. Cauls mouldy tripes windpipes faked and minced up. Puzzle find the meat. Kosher. No meat and milk together. Hygiene that was what they call now. Yom kippur fast spring cleaning of inside. Peace and war depend on some fellow's digestion. Religions. Christmas turkeys and geese. Slaughter of innocents. Eat, drink and be merry. Then casual wards after. Heads bandaged. Cheese digests all but itself. Mighty cheese.

Then comes the expected interruption of the flow. Bloom has arrived at a point which can now be expressed in action.

– Have you a cheese sandwich?
– Yes, sir.

In this same chapter, Joyce demonstrates how an incursion into genuine poetry can match the sexual elation of one of Bloom's memories. We are not, as it might seem, too far away from food. Joyce had the theory that wine arose through the fermentation of grapes in a woman's mouth, and the taste was first conveyed through a kiss:

Glowing wine on his palate lingered swallowed. Crushing in the winepress grapes of Burgundy. Sun's heat it is. Seems to a secret touch telling me memory. Touched his sense moistened remembered. Hidden under wild ferns on Howth. Below us bay sleeping sky. No sound. The sky. The bay purple by the Lion's head. Green by Drumleck. Yellowgreen towards Sutton. Fields of undersea, the lines faint brown in grass, buried cities. Pillowed on my coat she had her hair, earwigs in the heather scrub my hand under her nape, you'll toss me all. O wonder! Coolsoft with ointments her hand touched me, caressed: her eyes upon me did not turn away. Ravished over her I lay, full lips full open, kissed her mouth. Yum. Softly she gave me in my mouth the seedcake warm and chewed. Mawkish pulp her mouth had mumbled sweet and sour with spittle. Joy: I ate it: joy.

That 'O wonder!' has the memorability of any of the great ejaculations of literature, but we must not suppose that Bloom really says it: it is the verbal equivalent of a non-verbal ecstasy.

Despite frequent ellipsis of thought and syntax, Bloom's flow is never difficult to follow. But as the novel progresses Joyce allows ellipsis and a kind of specially invented lexis of the senses to overcome plain or near-plain communication. This happens in the 'Sirens' episode, where music – sound without sense – is threading into Bloom's monologue:

Bloom. Flood of warm jimjam lickitup secretness flowed to flow in music out, in desire, dark to lick flow, invading. Tipping her tepping her tapping her topping her. Tup. Pores to dilate dilating. Tup. The joy the feel the warm the. Tup. To pour o'er sluices pouring gushes. Flood, gush, flow, joygush, tupthrop. Now! Language of love.

And at the end of the chapter Bloom's viscera provide a tune of their own (something to do with that burgundy), accompanied by Robert Emmet's last words and the noise of a tram:

Seabloom, greaseabloom viewed last words. Softly. *When my country takes her place among.*
    Prrprr.
    Must be the bur.
    Fff. Oo. Rrpr.
    Nations of the earth. No-one behind. She's passed. *Then and not till then.* Tram. Kran, kran, kran. Good oppor. Coming. Krandlkrankran. I'm sure it's the burgund. Yes. One, two. *Let my epitaph be.* Karaaaaaaa. *Written. I have.*
    Pprrpffrrppfff.
    Done.

When Bloom, whom, unlike Earwicker, we only otherwise meet waking, touches the borders of a doze in the 'Nausicaa' episode, the language becomes unintelligible to anyone who has not read with attention up to that point:

O sweety all your little girlwhite up I saw dirty bracegirdle made me do love sticky we two naughty Grace darling she him half past the bed met him pike hoses frillies for Raoul to perfume your wife black hair heave under embon *señorita* young eyes Mulvey plump years dreams return tail end Agendath swoony lovey showed me her next year in drawers return next in her next her next.

These fragments all refer back to experiences of the day, beginning with the most recent – Bloom's act of autoeroticism on being permitted to see Gerty Macdowell's 'little girlwhite up'; a thought of the actress Ann Bracegirdle; the sight of a lighthouse and concomitant thoughts of Grace Darling; Molly's deformation of the word *metempsychosis* earlier that day; the book *Sweets of Sin* with its character Raoul; the unfaithful wife's frillies and 'heaving embonpoint' in the same novel; Martha Clifford's enquiry as to what perfume Bloom's wife uses; Molly as a girl in Gibraltar and her affair with Lieutenant Mulvey; a fragment of newspaper he saw when buying his pork kidney, with its advertisement put in by Agendath Netaim, the planter's company.

There is one curious instance, back in the 'Laestrygonians' section, of Bloom's carrying his interior monologue away from the reader and then bringing it back again. He wishes to visit the urinal; he goes off thinking of nymphs and goddesses:

Dribbling a quiet message from his bladder came to go to do not to do there to do. A man and ready he drained his glass to the lees and walked, to men too they gave themselves, manly conscious, lay with men lovers, a youth enjoyed her, to the yard.

This, incidentally, is a very interesting paragraph from the stylistic angle. In the first sentence Joyce contrives a verbal effect which conveys exactly the brief vacillation which accompanies the micturative message: do I have to go now or can I leave it till later I have to go now. It is hard to decide whether the sentence should be classified as part of the external récit or part of the stream of consciousness: the 'his' perhaps decides it for us, only – as in the sentence that follows – Joyce frequently combines the two aspects in the one statement. This next sentence, perhaps owing to the influence of the goddesses (they eat ambrosia and drink nectar; their statues in the library museum are visual 'aids to digestion': thus they fit into the food pattern of the chapter), almost explicitly turns Bloom into a classical hero. 'A man and ready' – cliché heroic; 'drained ... to the lees' – Tennyson's Ulysses; 'manly conscious' – Bloom is aware of his male organ, though not now, despite the final word 'yard', as a phallus. While he is away at his negative unheroic task, others talk about him: Davy Byrne (whose pub he is in), Nosey Flynn, Bantam Lyons, Paddy Leonard. Bloom returns, leaves the pub, and walks towards Dawson Street, 'his tongue brushing his teeth smooth. Something green it would have to be: spinach say. Then with those Röntgen rays searchlight you could.' This is the tail-end of a train of thought he has been pursuing in the urinal, whither the reader has not pursued him. Nevertheless we do not doubt that the stream of consciousness has been pounding busily away. This is a confidence trick that works.

Stephen's interior monologue begins on the very first page of the book. Buck Mulligan is parodying the mass:

He peered sideways up and gave a long low whistle of call, then paused awhile in rapt attention, his even white teeth glistening here and there with gold points. Chrysostomos. Two strong shrill whistles answered through the calm.

That 'Chrysostomos' is characteristic of Stephen. It means *goldenmouthed*, refers directly to Mulligan's dental fillings, but relates hagiographically to St John Chrysostomos the eloquent. Mulligan's middle name is St John (so is that of his real-life model, Oliver Gogarty); the presiding discipline of the chapter is theology. It is a totally verbal interior monologue that is starting, one proper to a poet. And yet Stephen, as he has already demonstrated in *A Portrait*, is capable of odd visionary visitations which have primarily nothing to do with words, though words come into them or even initiate them. The word *foetus* in *A Portrait*, carved on the desk of a medical lecture theatre, summons a vision of a student, very clearly seen, cutting the word with a knife, while other students laugh around him. A deformed man, lover of Sir Walter Scott, whom he talks to outside the National Library, is said to be the product of an incestuous union. Stephen sees the union taking place – brother and sister in an exactly visualised idyllic setting. Here in *Ulysses* he has a sudden image of an Oxford ragging, complete with soundtrack. This is followed by:

Shouts from the open window startling evening in the quadrangle. A deaf gardener, aproned, masked with Matthew Arnold's face, pushes his mower on the sombre lawn watching narrowly the dancing motes of grasshalms.

To ourselves ... new paganism ... omphalos.

Gogarty, as we learn from the Joyce biographies, talked of turning the Martello tower where he and Joyce actually lived for a time into the omphalos of a new Hellenism. We have moved from a visual image, through the Matthew Arnold mask, to Arnold's own writings and Mulligan-Gogarty's Wildean neopaganism.

Though, in this first chapter, Joyce gives Stephen the occasional flashed elliptical notation of thought or memory – 'Her glazing eyes, staring out of death, to shake and bend my soul. On me alone. The ghostcandle to light her agony. Ghostly light on her

tortured face –' he finds it more convenient for the purpose of
characterisation to shape a swift meditation into a piece of fine
writing, as when Stephen is thinking about the power of the
Church:

The proud potent titles clanged over Stephen's memory the triumph
of their brazen bells: *et unam sanctam catholicam et apostolicam ecclesiam*:
the slow growth and change of rite and dogma like his own rare
thoughts, a chemistry of stars. Symbol of the apostles in the mass for
pope Marcellus, the voices blended, singing alone loud in affirmation:
and behind their chant the vigilant angel of the church militant dis-
armed and menaced her heresiarchs. A horde of heresies fleeting with
mitres awry: Photius and the brood of mockers of whom Mulligan
was one, and Arius, warring his life long upon the consubstantiality
of the Son with the Father, and Valentine, spurning Christ's terrene
body, and the subtle African heresiarch Sabellius who held that the
Father was Himself His own Son. . . .

And in the 'Proteus' chapter, where he brings theology to a point
that will prove relevant to his filial relationship to Bloom:

Wombed in sin darkness I was too, made not begotten. By them, the
man with my voice and my eyes and a ghostwoman with ashes on her
breath. They clasped and sundered, did the coupler's will. From before
the ages He willed me and now may not will me away or ever. A
lex eterna stays about him. Is that then the divine substance wherein
Father and Son are consubstantial? Where is poor dear Arius to try
conclusions? Warring his life long on the contransmagnificandjewbang-
tantiality . . .

That final ghastly portmanteau reminds us that it is no longer
theology that presides but the secular art of philology. The very
loose connection with the Odyssey is made through Proteus
(whom Menelaus tried to bind, not Telemachus). The slippery,
elusive, primal living substance, always ready to change its shape,
is figured in language – especially language as Joyce uses it. The
chapter is full of loanwords, calques, neologisms, as well as curious learning: as we are as far away from the down-to-earth broodings of Bloom as it is possible to imagine. Bloom, of course, we
have not yet met, and we fearsomely expect that all streams of
consciousness are going to be something like this:

Ineluctable modality of the visible: at least that if no more, thought
through my eyes. Signatures of all things I am here to read, seaspawn

and seawrack, the nearing tide, that rusty boot. Snotgreen, bluesilver, rust: coloured signs. Limits of the diaphane. But he adds: in bodies. Then he was aware of them bodies before of them coloured. How? By knocking his sconce against them, sure. Go easy. Bald he was and a millionaire, *maestro di color che sanno*. Limit of the diaphane in. Why in? Diaphane, adiaphane. If you can put your five fingers through it, it is a gate, if not a door. Shut your eyes and see.

The ellipsis here is more in the thought than the language (though it is there too: 'aware of them bodies before of them coloured'). We have to know something of Aristotle – whom Dante called 'master of them that know' – before we can follow Stephen. But the long monologue that makes up the chapter is not all heavy learning. Stephen can swoop down to a colloquialism:

By knocking his sconce against them, sure.
Papa's little bedpal. Lump of love.
Shoot him to bloody bits with a bang shotgun . . .
A woman and a man. I see her skirties. Pinned up, I bet.

This last would do well enough for Bloom. There is humour and playfulness and self-mockery, and these are ice-cool foils to the poetic turgidity:

Under the upswelling tide he saw the writhing weeds lift languidly and sway reluctant arms, hising up their petticoats, in whispering water swaying and upturning coy silver fronds. Day by day: night by night; lifted, flooded and let fall. Lord, they are weary: and, whispered to, they sigh. Saint Ambrose heard it, sigh of leaves and waves, waiting, awaiting the fullness of their times, *diebus ac noctibus iniurias patiens ingemiscit*. To no end gathered: vainly then released, forth flowering, wending back: loom of the moon. Weary too in sight of lovers, lascivious men, a naked woman shining in her courts, she draws a toil of waters.

The heavy beauty of that is lightened by two comic references. In the first chapter Mulligan sings a coarse song about old Mary Ann who doesn't give a damn but hising up her petticoats . . . The 'lascivious' goes back a page or so to Stephen's memory of:

The froeken, *bonne à tout faire*, who rubs male nakedness in the bath at Upsala. *Moi faire*, she said. *Tous les messieurs*. Not this *Monsieur*, I said. Most licentious custom. Bath a most private thing. I wouldn't let my brother, not even my own brother, most lascivious thing. Green eyes, I see you. Fang, I feel. Lascivious people.

The 'Proteus' chapter ends the *Telemachia*, after which Stephen-Telemachus must take a back seat while Ulysses-Bloom rules over the bulk of the book. When we meet Stephen's interior mono-loguising again, it is much subdued, though, in the intervals of lecturing on Shakespeare in the National Library, he is capable of highly wrought unspoken ejaculations as well as a very moving piece of blasphemy (the influence of the art of the first chapter is very potent):

He Who Himself begot, middler the Holy Ghost, and Himself sent himself, Agenbuyer, between Himself and others, Who, put upon by His fiends, stripped and whipped, was nailed like bat to barndoor, starved on crosstree, Who let Him bury, stood up, harrowed hell, fared into heaven and there these nineteen hundred years sitteth on the right hand of His Own Self but yet shall come in the latter day to doom the quick and dead when all the quick shall be dead already.

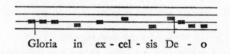

Gloria   in   ex - cel - sis De - o

This, of course, offends every conceivable canon of realism. That mockcreed has to be verbally expressed, but no mind, however dedally brilliant, can improvise it. The artificiality of the passage is emphasised by the music of the plainchant Gloria, presented in archaic notation. It relieves the eye, newspaper McLuhan, but otherwise points to self-indulgence more than stern Flaubertian fictionalising. The Photian credo can only be justified as a liturgical balancing of the blasphemous British-navy doxology that comes in the 'Cyclops' chapter (see Chapter 11).

The final monologue of Molly Bloom, though rightly praised as astonishing insight into a woman's mind and one of the most heartening yea-saying pieces in all literature, is not so original as it looks.

Really so sorry that I should happen to be late on this morning of all mornings because my intention and my wish was to be ready to meet you when you came in and to say that any one that interested Arthur Clennam half so much must interest me and that I gave you the heartiest welcome and was so glad, instead of which they never called me and there I still am snoring I dare say if the truth was known and if you don't like either cold fowl or hot boiled ham which many people don't

I dare say besides Jews and theirs are scruples of conscience which we must all respect though I must say I wish they had them equally strong when they sell us false articles for real that certainly ain't worth the money I shall be quite vexed.

The above is a speech of Flora Finching's in *Little Dorrit*. It is a good deal more confusing than anything in Molly's self-communing, but it is shorter, and the confusedness is part of Dickens's intention. Here is Molly, with punctuation restored:

O wasn't I the born fool to believe all his blather about Home Rule and the Land League, sending me that long strool of a song out of *The Huguenots* to sing in French, to be more classy – 'O beau pays de la Touraine' – that I never even sang once, explaining and rigmaroling about religion and persecution – he won't let you enjoy anything naturally – then might he as a great favour – The very first opportunity he got a chance in Brighton Square, running into my bedroom pretending the ink got on his hands to wash it off with the Albion milk and sulphur soap I used to use, and the gelatine still round it. O I laughed myself sick at him that day. I'd better not make an all-night sitting on this affair. They ought to make chambers a natural size so that a woman could sit on it properly. He kneels down to do it. I suppose there isn't in all creation another man with the habits he has.

It looks less avant-garde set in this orthodox manner. Molly's syntax gets garbled, sentence is jammed into sentence, but on the whole the presentation of her thoughts is orderly, even literary, and we end seeing the huge chapter as an ideally long letter from Nora Joyce. The interior monologues of Bloom and Stephen represent a genuine technical advance in the externalisation of the internal, but it was only the lack of punctuation in the 'Penelope' chapter that made its first readers see frightening modernity.

Molly, like Stephen and Bloom, is free to touch areas of thought once inadmissible in literature – inadmissible, indeed, in this very book: it was the final chapter more than any that excited the censors. But she is no more free than they to wander precisely where she wishes. Joyce makes her Gea-Tellus and forces her to take up temporary symbolic positions where she exemplifies the history of the earth, stage by geological stage. The fire inside her gushes out; there was a terribly cold ice-age winter when she played with little dolls (primordial men); she loves the mornings when the world is deserted; she is passionate for flowers; for her there is nothing like nature. But the general impression – and, of course, it is not one to grumble about – is of a free feminine fantasy set down in automatism on paper, or transcribed from a tape as big as a cartweel.

Joyce is close to Dickensian techniques of character-presentation in three other places – all contained in the 'Wandering Rocks' episode. Father Conmee S.J. begins this section, and the viceregal cavalcade ends it, so that we have the impression of two safe shores – church and state – between which the barques of Dublin citizenry sail. Father Conmee's mild firmness is an aspect of his office; he is an impersonal agent of the Church; his dreams and tastes touch no deep level of idiosyncrasy:

Don John Conmee walked and moved in times of yore. He was humane and honoured there. He bore in mind secrets confessed and he smiled at smiling noble faces in a beeswaxed drawingroom, ceiled with full fruit clusters. And the hands of a bride and bridegroom, noble to noble, were impalmed by don John Conmee.
It was a charming day.
The lychgate of a field showed Father Conmee breadths of cabbages, curtseying to him with ample underleaves. The sky showed him a flock of small white clouds going slowly down the wind. *Moutonner*, the French said. A homely and just word.

Nature, as well as Dublin, defers to Father Conmee. The technique is charming and wholly Dickensian. A first-person interior monologue would be overpresumptuous; keep to the third person and he remains a priest, not a man:

Father Conmee perceived her perfume in the car. He perceived also that the awkward man at the other side of her was sitting on the edge of the seat.
Father Conmee at the altarrails placed the host with difficulty in the mouth of the awkward old man who had the shaky head.

Mr Kernan, for no clear reason, is permitted to disclose his inner thoughts:

Mr Kernan halted and preened himself before the sloping mirror of Peter Kennedy, hairdresser. Stylish coat, beyond a doubt. Scott of Dawson street. Well worth the half sovereign I gave Neary for it. Never built under three guineas. Fits me down to the ground. Some Kildare street club toff had it probably. John Mulligan, the manager of the Hibernian bank, gave me a very sharp eye yesterday on Carlisle bridge as if he remembered me.

And Master Patrick Aloysius Dignam, whose father was buried that morning with Mr Bloom as one of the mourners, thinks about the coffin that was bumped down the stairs:

Pa was inside it and ma crying in the parlour and uncle Barney telling the men how to get it round the bend. A big coffin it was, and high and heavylooking. How was that? The last night pa was boosed he was standing on the landing there bawling out for his boots to go out to Tunney's for to boose more and he looked butty and short in his shirt. Never see him again. Death, that is. Pa is dead. My father is dead. He told me to be a good son to ma. I couldn't hear the other things he said but I saw his tongue and his teeth trying to say it better. Poor pa. That was Mr Dignam, my father. I hope he is in purgatory now because he went to confession to father Conroy on Saturday night.

These brief interior monologues could quite easily, if there were a sympathetic interlocutor present, be direct speech: there are none of the ellipses which characterise the inner musings of Bloom and Stephen. They represent an intermediate stage between speech and thought and suggest what is so often found in Dickens – stream-of-consciousness language which becomes comic by being externalised. Mrs Nickleby provides some good examples:

I remember when your poor papa and I came to town after we were married, that a young lady brought me home a chip cottage-bonnet, with white and green trimming, and green persian lining, in her own carriage, which drove up to the door full gallop; – at least, I am not quite certain whether it was her own carriage or a hackney chariot, but I remember very well that the horse dropped down dead as he was turning round, and that your poor papa said he hadn't had any corn for a fortnight.

Joyce exhausted the possibilities of interior monologue, as of so many other literary techniques, in *Ulysses*, and it cannot be said that any of his followers* have used the innovation with success. Gulley Jimson, in Joyce Cary's *The Horse's Mouth*, sounds like Bloom, and the only alternative was to make him sound like Stephen. To employ the technique with the same boldness as Joyce means to use the same devices of control and limitation, which means to write another *Ulysses*. One *Ulysses* is probably enough.

* Except William Faulkner, but it is hard to see him as a follower.

CHAPTER 5

The Joyce Sentence

𝕾𝕾𝕾𝕾𝕾𝕾

THE material of the few score pages which make up the final chapter of *A Portrait* is a distillation of hundreds of pages of a book called *Stephen Hero*. This was Joyce's first attempt at recording his own life in novel-form, and all we have of this juvenile effort is the section dealing with Stephen Dedalus's university days – written, much of it, while the events dramatised were actually taking place. The whitehot immediacy is what gives the fragment interest, and the appetite for notation – pinning conversation down on paper while it is still breathing – is the essence of Joyce, young or old. We need not regret overmuch the disappearance of the earlier sections of the manuscript; what we have teaches us all we wish to know about the development of the artist trying to free himself from the toils of fictional tradition and revolutionise the novel-form. Here is a specimen of the prose of the very early Joyce:

As Stephen looked at the big square block of masonry looming before them through the faint daylight, he re-entered again in thought the seminarist life which he had led for so many years, to the understanding of the narrow activities of which he could now in a moment bring the spirit of an acute sympathetic alien. He recognised at once the martial mind of the Irish Church in the style of this ecclesiastical barracks. He looked in vain at the faces and figures which passed him for a token of moral elevation: all were cowed without being humble, modish without being simple-mannered.

This is very decent writing, assured, literary, and it represents a style that still serves certain major names in British and American fiction. But Joyce, seventy years ago, recognised that it was already old-fashioned. It did not match the subject-matter: it was a cloak rather than a skintight garment. To think in terms of a general prose-style suitable for all aspects of fictional material was the old way. James and Conrad and Hardy found their mature style and stuck to it; what Joyce wanted was the ability to create any number of different styles, each appropriate to its own subject-matter and to that only. He recognised that critics and ordinary readers were not ready for such an innovation. What would they make, for instance, of the opening to *A Portrait of the Artist as a Young Man*?

Once upon a time and a very good time it was there was a moocow coming down along the road and this moocow that was coming down along the road met a nicens little boy named baby tuckoo . . . .

There are still critics and ordinary readers who would much prefer the novel to begin like this:

My earliest recollections are of my father and my mother bending over my cot and of the difference in personal odour that subsisted between my two parents. My father, certainly, did not have so pleasant an odour as my mother. I remember I would be told infantile stories, altogether appropriate to my infantile station. One of them, I seem to recall, was concerned with a cow coming down the lane – which lane was never specified – and meeting a child who was called (I am embarrassed, inevitably, to recollect this in maturity) some such name as Baby Tuckoo. I myself, apparently, was to be thought of as Baby Tuckoo. Or was it Cuckoo? It is, of course, so long ago . . .

Most of us take the Joycean immediacy for granted now, but where the technique is not so spectacular, as in the volume of short stories *Dubliners*, we occasionally have to shake ourselves out of the false conviction that this prose-style of 'scrupulous meanness' (Joyce's own term) is a dead and dull and inept way of writing. The earlier stories, which deal with childhood, have a kind of lift about them, a quality of excitement, wonder, and romantic yearning, as in the first, 'The Sisters', where the word 'paralysis' (keyword for the whole volume) fascinates the young narrator:

Every night as I gazed up at the window I said softly to myself the word paralysis. It had always sounded strangely in my ears, like the word gnomon in the Euclid and the word simony in the Catechism. But now it sounded to me like the name of some maleficent and sinful being. It filled me with fear, and yet I longed to be nearer to it and to look upon its deadly work.

Or the second, 'An Encounter', in which two young boys meet

a shabby little man, full of perverse fantasies, who indulges in a monologue about how he would whip any boy who had a sweetheart:

He described to me how he would whip such a boy, as if he were unfolding some elaborate mystery. He would love that, he said, better than anything in this world; and his voice, as he led me monotonously through the mystery, grew almost affectionate and seemed to plead with me that I should understand him.

Or 'Araby', where a pubescent boy is learning about love's bitter mystery:

I imagined that I bore my chalice safely through a throng of foes. Her name sprang to my lips at moments in strange prayers and praises which I myself did not understand.

Thwarted of buying a promised present for his beloved – he is late getting to the bazaar called Araby (held in Dublin May 14 to 19, 1894, in aid of Jervis Street Hospital); it is just closing down – he expresses his frustration thus to himself:

Gazing up into the darkness I saw myself as a creature driven and derided by vanity; and my eyes burned with anguish and anger.

But, when we enter the adult world, the frustrations and paralyses attendant on the lives of the drab Dubliners need a prose that never flowers into passion or complexity. Everything is set down exactly but coldly, even with a deliberate touch of cliché. In 'After the Race' the racingcars come 'scudding in towards Dublin, running evenly like pellets in the groove of the Naas Road':

At the crest of the hill at Inchicore sightseers had gathered in clumps to watch the cars careering homeward, and through this channel of poverty and inaction the Continent had sped its wealth and industry. Now and again the clumps of people raised the cheer of the gratefully oppressed . . .

At the opening of 'Grace', Mr Kernan re-enacts the fall of man:

Two gentlemen who were in the lavatory at the time tried to lift him up: but he was quite helpless. He lay curled up at the foot of the stairs down which he had fallen. They succeeded in turning him over. His hat had rolled a few yards away and his clothes were smeared with the filth and ooze of the floor on which he had lain, face downwards. His eyes were closed and he breathed with a grunting noise. A thin stream of blood trickled from the corner of his mouth.

The style maintains a flatness which avoids the rhythmical lift of the author's own response – compassion or disgust or even superior facetiousness. The over-all effect of the prose of *Dubliners* is grey. Only in the final story 'The Dead' – an afterthought which would never have got into the book if the delay between writing and publication had not been so great – do we touch regions of mystery and magic, but even there the prose remains impartial and flat, resigning emotional complexity to the symbols – snow all over Ireland, a grave in Galway – and to the words of speech or thought.

It is Joyce's search for an objective prose-style that concerns us – a récit which shall be as close as possible to the subject-matter and from which the personality of the writer is totally excluded. Obviously this means a sort of trickery, since the author is always there, expressing himself through the choice of language and rhythm, the very impartiality. But whereas traditional fiction assumed that the novelist should be present in every scene, commenting, colouring, judging, behaving like God, the post-Flaubertian way was to serve realism by giving the reader the illusion that he was observing life directly, without the artist's embarrassing intermediacy. In *Dubliners* Joyce is withdrawn; we cannot point to an implied comment on the action or to an idiosyncratic mode of description which gives us a sudden flashlight portrait of the artist. Objectivity is achieved.

In *A Portrait* Joyce is writing only about himself – though we should not assume that the work lacks invention, that Stephen Dedalus is no more than a photograph of his creator. The stylistic problem seems to resolve itself into a need for finding tones, rhythm and lexis appropriate to the young hero at each stage of his growth from infancy to maturity. And so we move from 'baby tuckoo' to a young schoolboy who wonders about adult politics and fails to understand them:

He wondered which was right, to be for the green or for the maroon, because Dante had ripped the green velvet back off the brush that was for Parnell one day with her scissors and had told him that Parnell was a bad man. He wondered if they were arguing at home about that. That was called politics. There were two sides in it: Dante was on one side and his father and Mr Casey were on the other side but his mother and Uncle Charles were on no side.

The simple words, the simple constructions, the naive repetitions are all in order. But, as Stephen grows a little older, subordinate clauses appear, and the vocabulary admits abstractions:

Words which he did not understand he said over and over to himself till he had learnt them by heart; and through them he had glimpses of the real world about him. The hour when he too would take part in the life of that world seemed drawing near and in secret he began to make ready for the great part which he felt awaited him the nature of which he only dimly apprehended.

'The nature of which he only dimly apprehended': evidently Stephen is reading nineteenth-century literature of the staider kind. The movement forward from stage to stage of youth is not smoothly evolutionary: the soul has to be shocked, chiefly through the body, to jerk or jump ahead. Stephen, whose glasses have been broken, is accused of breaking them himself to avoid schoolwork and is beaten by the Prefect of Studies with a pandy-bat:

A hot burning stinging tingling blow like the loud crack of a broken stick made his trembling hand crumple together like a leaf in the fire: and at the sound and the pain scalding tears were driven into his eyes. His whole body was shaking with fright, his arm was shaking and his crumpled burning livid hand shook like a loose leaf in the air. A cry sprang to his lips, a prayer to be let off. But though the tears scalded his eyes and his limbs quivered with pain and fright he held back the hot tears and the cry that scalded his throat.
  – Other hand! shouted the prefect of studies.

The power of this is undoubted, but the source of the power is not easy to explain: magic remains a genuine property of art. Still, one ought to observe that much of the excruciating effect springs from objectivity, from an unwillingness to allow the author's own indignation to intrude. Then there is the elemental simplicity of the vocabulary, which emphasises the elemental shock of the pain. There is no finicking attempt to vary the words used: 'scald' appears three times, an apt word worthy to be repeated, since it combines the elements of fire and water. Stephen's passivity is pointed by the two references to his hand as a leaf – once in the fire, once in the third element, air. The pandybat sounds like a stick, but it is a broken stick that could also be in the fire along with the leaf: the experience of pain cannot separate the pain from its cause. The passivity is present in his tears: he does not cry – which seems like performing an action; the tears are 'driven into his eyes'. He does not wish to cry out: the cry springs to his lips. The onomatopoeic effects need hardly be commented on. Repeated vowels and consonants express the noise of the pandybat, but the manner in which the agony of the blow seems to take possession of the entire universe is conveyed by the swift vocalic leaps, as though the pain were rushing from the centre to all possible spatial positions.

Thus, in the first sentence, we dart from the back round close vowel in 'hot' to the slack central vowel of 'burning,' then up to the high front slack vowel which is used five times successively, back to the round diphthong of 'blow,' down to the rising diphthong of 'like,' and so on. The sentence contains all the vowels except /ɑː/ and /uː/, five diphthongs, and the triphthong (though this may not be in everyone's phonemic inventory) in 'fire.' This is not in itself remarkable, but the manner in which diverse tongue-and-lip positions are juxtaposed certainly gives a ghastly vigour to the passage.

The technique of *Ulysses* is foreshadowed at two points in the narrative of the chapter where Stephen is mature enough to have fallen into deep sin and experiences spiritual torments which breed hallucinations. Faces watch him and voices murmur:

– We knew perfectly well of course that although it was bound to come to the light he would find considerable difficulty in endeavouring to try to induce himself to try to endeavour to ascertain the spiritual plenipotentiary and so we knew of course perfectly well –

The vision of hell is almost a stage direction from 'Circe':

A field of stiff weeds and thistles and tufted nettlebunches. Thick among the tufts of rank stiff growth lay battered canisters and clots and coils of solid excrement. A faint marsh light struggling upwards from all the ordure through the bristling greygreen weeds. An evil smell, faint and foul as the light, curled upward sluggishly out of the canisters and from the stale crusted dung.

We note here what we will note in *Ulysses*: Joyce's preference for a compound word over a noun-phrase ('nettlebunches' instead of 'bunches of nettles'); his liking for an adjective-phrase followed by inversion of subject and verb ('Thick among the tufts of rank stiff growth lay battered canisters . . .'); his insistence on a vocabulary of Anglo-Saxon origin when presenting material directed at the senses. ('Canister' is from Latin *canistrum*; its use here is probably part-dictated by the ecclesiastical connotation, since a canister is the vessel that holds the wafers before they are consecrated. 'Excrement' is preferred to *shit* or *shite*, but Joyce intends to make the latter word express the ultimate nausea of the vision.) Again, the prosodic technique is masterly. The 'clotted' effect partly derives from the double consonants – /ld/, /dz/, /ft/, /nʃ/ and so on – and occasional triple consonants: /slz/, /fts/, /kskr/ in 'excrement' (a tougher word than any Anglo-Saxon equivalent).

When Stephen emerges into the fair fields of penitent purity, the prose becomes unexpectedly pedestrian, to match the failure of the young soul to find the ecstasy it hoped for in virtue and mortification of the flesh:

He seemed to feel his soul in devotion pressing like fingers the keyboard of a great cash register and to see the amount of his purchase start forth immediately in heaven, not as a number but as a frail column of incense or as a slender flower.

But when he realises that his vocation is to be a sinning artist, he has a new vision, that of a winged form over the sea, slowly mounting the sky – his protonym Daedalus, the fabulous artificer. The prose that conveys his ecstatic state balances the Anglo-Saxon and Latin elements of English; the syntax becomes simple, almost childish, to match the sense of being newborn:

His heart trembled in an ecstasy of fear and his soul was in flight. His soul was soaring in an air beyond the world and the body he knew was purified in a breath and delivered of incertitude and made radiant and commingled with the element of the spirit. An ecstasy of flight made radiant his eyes and wild his breath and tremulous and wild and radiant his windswept limbs.

This is expressive of a somewhat immature transport: after all, Stephen is still a schoolboy. It is the prose appropriate to a youth who has read Shelley but is not yet ready for either Donne or Rabelais.

The final section of the novel, in which Stephen is presented as a rebellious undergraduate unsympathetic to philistine, religiose Ireland, a fierce young artist and aesthetic philosopher who has left the Church and is preparing to leave the country, anticipates stylistically the first chapter of *Ulysses*. The important things are less what Stephen does than what he says; we come close to monologue, in which the outside world that has menaced him so long is at last enclosed and tamed by his mind. It is at the end of the novel that we realise how thoroughgoing Joyce's objectivity has been. The mature artist has never once stepped in to qualify the attitudes of the young soul struggling unconsciously towards a vocation. The undergraduate Stephen is old enough for the creator Joyce to be tempted into an identification, but the mind that is brilliant enough for the disquisition on aesthetics is also adolescent enough for *fin-de-siècle* postures of 'weariness' and for a brash unlikeable dogmatism that Joyce neither condones nor condemns. The book ends with diary entries which, in their elliptical irritability, self-mockery, fearless lyricism, look forward to the 'Proteus' episode of *Ulysses*, but, in their lack of syntax and flashes of discrete observation, recall the opening with 'baby tuckoo' and his attempts to make a gestalt out of smells and hot and cold and wet and dry. The cutting of the physical umbilical cord is matched by the cutting of the spiritual. 'Welcome, O life!' cries the artist as a young man, and he goes forth 'to forge in the smithy of my soul the uncreated conscience of my race'.

One of the aesthetic problems of *Ulysses* was to find a prose-style that should be as impersonal as the one of *Dubliners* but, in deference to the heroic symbolism of the book, should be not drab and grey and paralytic but poetic if laconic, specific and exact but also ringing with harmonics. A great deal of the novel is carried by interior monologue, or by the narrative of personal or non-personal observers, or by parody and pastiche, but there are odd corners of the récit that call for the artist to present his own statement, richly but in total self-effacement. Let us look at the very opening. Buck Mulligan is presented to us immediately, not through the mind of Stephen Dedalus, who is still to come up the stairs of the Martello tower into the bright June morning:

Stately, plump Buck Mulligan came from the stairhead, bearing a bowl of lather on which a mirror and a razor lay crossed. A yellow dressing-gown, ungirdled, was sustained gently behind him by the mild morning air. He held the bowl aloft and intoned:
   – *Introibo ad altare Dei.*
Halted, he peered down the dark winding stairs and called up coarsely:

– Come up, Kinch. Come up, you fearful jesuit.

Solemnly he came forward and mounted the round gunrest. He faced about and blessed gravely thrice the tower, the surrounding country and the awaking mountains.

We recognise at once some of the devices of brevity which Joyce has already used in *A Portrait*, particularly the preference for a single word over a phrase or clause, even when (or sometimes because) the effect is slightly archaic. Most writers today would substitute 'in the air' for its Old Norse equivalent (*a* – on, to – + *loft* – sky, cognate with German *Luft*). *Thrice* is not now much used, except facetiously, and it could be objected that a saving of one word is too inconsiderable to matter. Yet something is wrong with this editing: '. . . blessed gravely three times the tower, the surrounding country . . .' The headrhyme is non-functional and the word-order sounds eccentric. We would expect: 'gravely blessed the tower three times, also the surrounding country . . .' Joyce is fond of placing a modifier immediately after a transitive verb, but usually when it is a single word and not a phrase. For 'a yellow dressing-gown, ungirdled' many writers would substitute 'an ungirdled yellow dressing-gown', but Joyce's usage implies a pattern of wider import: 'ungirdled' suggests the truncation of an adjective phrase or clause coming naturally after the noun. To justify the postposition, many would be tempted to rewrite as 'which he wore ungirdled' or 'which had no girdle'.

The whole opening passage suggests the mock-ceremonial (the presiding art is, we have to remember, theology). The very first word, 'stately' is comic as applied to Mulligan, who is coarse and blasphemous as well as plump. (Sometimes, though no dictionary condones such usage, one wonders if Joyce meant it adverbially.) We hear the same vowel /ʌ/ three times, or thrice, in 'plump Buck Mulligan', suggesting the repeated note of the opening of some ceremonial plainchant. 'Bearing a bowl' for the Class 1 novelist's 'carrying a bowl' exploits headrhyme in the service of the mock-poetic, meaning the mock-liturgical (incidentally, how does one cross a mirror and a razor?). The long vowels and diphthongs of the second sentence – /aʊ/, /ɜː/, /eɪ/, /aɪ/, /ɔː/, /ɛə/ – keep the pace appropriately slow and stately. There is a faded poeticism in the phrase 'the awaking mountains' which is strangely fitting, especially as it comes in a context of prosodic mockery: between 'Solemnly' and the end of the citation the diphthong /aʊ/ appears six times. It serves to bind all the elements of Mulligan's mock-blessing into one, it echoes the repeated-note plainchant effect of 'plump Buck Mulligan', it even suggests Mulligan's stoutness.

Joyce has, it seems to me, very successfully imparted to his opening a sort of mock-bardic impersonality which has an heroic counterpart in the conventional epic tones of antiquity. He achieves a different kind of success in the following much-quoted passage from the 'Proteus' chapter:

The grainy sand had gone from under his feet. His boots trod again a damp crackling mast, razorshells, squeaking pebbles, that on the unnumbered pebbles beats, wood sieved by the shipworm, lost Armada. Unwholesome sandflats waited to suck his treading soles, breathing upward sewage breath. He coasted them, walking warily. A porterbottle stood up, stogged to its waist, in the cakey sand dough. A sentinel: isle of dreadful thirst. Broken hoops on the shore; at the land a maze of dark cunning nets; farther away chalkscrawled backdoors and on the higher beach a dryingline with two crucified shirts. Ringsend: wigwams of brown steersmen and master mariners. Human shells.

The reader's skill is first engaged in separating the elements of Stephen's interior monologue from the third-person narration: they are very cunningly knitted into each other. But the Joyce descriptive technique is clearly in evidence. The vocabulary, for instance, is almost totally Anglo-Saxon; even the few words of Romance origin have long been assimilated to the language. There are a few surprises – 'mast' properly means the fruit of foresttrees, especially as food for swine; 'sewage' is admirably used as an adjective, as is 'sand' in 'cakey sand dough'; 'stogged' is exactly right; the compounds – 'razorshells', 'sandflats', 'chalkscrawled' and the rest – have the effect of emphasising the Teutonic basis of the vocabulary, essential in a piece of description of a northern littoral. The task of relating the elemental *données* to the current of human life is left to Stephen who, typically, does it through literature. 'Walking warily' brings Stephen and the narrator together. It can be glossed as a poeticism or near-archasim or as a Shakespeareanism: Shakespeare is never far from Stephen's mind.

The hero of the novel is introduced in what seems to be the kind of generalisation beloved of traditional fiction:

Mr Leopold Bloom ate with relish the inner organs of beasts and fowls. He liked thick giblet soup, nutty gizzards, a stuffed roast heart, liver slices fried with crustcrumbs, fried hencod's roes. Most of all he liked grilled mutton kidneys which gave to his palate a fine tang of faintly scented urine.

Most of the key-words here are short-vowelled – 'ate', 'relish', 'inner', 'thick giblet', 'nutty gizzards', 'stuffed', 'liver', 'crust-crumbs', 'hencod's' – suggesting probably a briskness and practicality absent from such a passage as this from the first chapter, built as it is out of long vowels and diphthongs:

Woodshadows floated silently by through the morning peace from the stairhead seaward where he gazed. Inshore and farther out the mirror of water whitened, spurned by lightshod hurrying feet. White breast of the dim sea. The twining stresses, two by two. A hand plucking the harpstrings merging their twining chords. Wavewhite wedded words shimmering on the dim tide.

Wavewhite wedded words for Stephen; kidneys for Bloom.

There is as much faint mockery in this opening to the Bloom-Odyssey proper as there is in the opening to the book itself. If Mulligan celebrates a parodic mass, Bloom, more classically, consults viscera. 'Beasts' recall the beasts of the field and 'fowls' the fowls of the air: the tone is vaguely biblical. The concentration on inner organs is appropriate in other ways. This chapter corresponds to the Calypso episode of the Odyssey. Mrs Molly Bloom is Penelope only at the end of the book; here she is the nymph who belongs to an island with a great cave at its centre (Gibraltar too has its caves) and who, in a sense, detains Bloom in her abode. His ancestral home is in the East, but she has him firmly anchored in the West. The chapter is full of caves – Molly's own dark bed-room, the outdoor lavatory, the black suit Bloom wears for the funeral, the body itself (which we can leave only through metem-psychosis or met him pike hoses). If we wander through the caves of the body we shall meet giblets, a heart, gizzards, liver and kidneys. A kidney is the bodily organ which rules the chapter (the body has not been celebrated at all in the Telemachia: Stephen is pure imagination, raised above the flesh). The science which controls the action is economics, the useful art of house-hold management: inner organs – useful and essential but far from poetic – subterraneously drudge away in the service of the body's economy. Bloom is essential gut; Stephen essential intellect. That opening paragraph is no mere whimsy.

It is a highly organised piece of writing, in which the dishes made of lowly organs are expressed through succulent consonants. 'Crustcrumbs' taste better than mere *breadcrumbs*. The *hen* of 'hencod's' is supererogatory, since only hencods have roes, but it is a thickening element which relates fish to fowl. The 'fine tang of faintly scented urine' – disgusting to some readers – is down to earth and makes the kidney functional as well as esculent. Again, this is a completely impersonal but highly flavoursome piece of writing, in which the sonic organisation is highly distinguished and the lexis is apt.

As the narrative of the Bloom Odyssey proceeds, more work is given to interior monologue than to external description, but Joyce makes use pretty consistently of brief statements made from the angle of an impersonal observer to punctuate the stream of Bloom's thought and feeling. Here are some examples from the lotus-eating chapter:

1. By Brady's cottages a boy for the skins lolled, his bucket of offal linked, smoking a chewed fagbutt.
2. A smaller girl with scars of eczema on her forehead eyed him, listlessly holding her battered caskhoop.
3. Under their dropped lids his eyes found the tiny bow of the leather headband inside his high grade ha.
4. He came nearer and heard a crunching of gilded oats, the gently champing teeth.
5. A wise tabby, a blinking sphinx, watched from her warm sill.
6. Weak joy opened his lips.
7. The bungholes sprang open and a huge dull flood leaked out, flowing together, winding through mudflats all over the level land, a lazy pooling swirl of liquor bearing along wideleaved flowers of its froth.
8. The cold smell of sacred stone called him.
9. He waited by the counter, inhaling the keen reek of drugs, the dusty dry smell of sponges and loofahs.
10. He foresaw his pale body reclined in it at full, naked, in a womb of warmth, oiled by scented melting soap, softly laved.

Probably a reader sensitive to language, knowing something of modern literature, though nothing yet of Joyce, would recognise a common quality in these ten sentences – not the revelation of a personality so much as evidence of a distinctive approach to what might be termed literary engineering. In the first place, each sentence seems to play a tune independent of the sense. It is as if Joyce were given a keyboard capable of striking all the English vowel phonemes and he at once began to play as many different ones as he could, leaping in wide intervals rather than treading a scale. Even where vowel-sounds are used to fine onomatopoeic effect, as in examples 7 and 10, there is still the instinct to move rapidly from a high tongue-position to a low, a front to a back, with a concomitant rapid spreading and rounding of the lips. There is perhaps the genuine influence of song here – literary language as something orally athletic. Joyce was brought up on *bel canto* – a truth hidden in Italian dialogue in the 'Wandering Rocks' chapter – and, though without professional phonetic training, he knew all about the production of vowels in singing. 'Smoking a chewed fagbutt' – the movement is from a close back diphthong to a close back vowel, very round, and then to a low front unrounded vowel, then to a back middle unrounded one. The tune does not really match the thing described – *smoking a cigarette-end* would get it as well – but there is a curiously impersonal quality about it, as though an instrument were playing: it is the impersonality, of course, that Joyce requires.

In every sentence there is a small lexical surprise – language behaving a fraction more unexpectedly than we would find in a Class 1 novelist. 'For the skins' is colloquial; so, I think is 'linked', though I was brought up on the term as meaning *held by the arm*; 'fagbutt' is certainly colloquial: the terms are appropriate to the Dublin boy described, but we probably expected either language fitting for Bloom's thoughts or a neutrality of vocabulary giving something like: 'A boy sent to collect pelts waited languidly outside Brady's cottages with his arm through the handle of a bucket of animal offal; he was smoking a cigarette-end.' In example 2 the 'caskhoop' surprises because it looks like a coinage, whereas it is only a swift version of 'hoop that had originally bound a cask'. The 'ha' in 3 we first meet in the 'Calypso' chapter: presumably sweat or grime has erased the original final letter of the legend on the hatband. It has been remarked that, while most characters in fiction possess a hat, Bloom is the only one to have a ha. It is the poetic 'gilded' of 4 that surprises: the epithet is not needed, especially as the oats are, presumably, not visible, but it fits the lotus-eating mood, elevating even horse-fodder to a sybaritic status. Example 5 is a small triumph of compression. Expanded to normal length, it would read: 'A tabby-cat watched blinking from a warm window-sill; she looked as wise as the Sphinx.' The attribution of sphingine wisdom through sly metaphor is comic, so is the rhyme hidden by ortho-graphy – /blɪŋk – sfɪŋk/ – as well as the faint gust of ambiguity in 'blinking' (a mild British intensive, euphemistic for *bloody*). But a more mysterious source of satisfaction is the sense of a brief rounded melody, functioning independently of semantic content. Example 6 shows Joyce's willingness to use an epithet which, in a human context, implies a value-judgment, as a mere impersonal indicator of degree. In 7 we should note that the choice of 'wideleaved flowers' is suggested by the floral motif of the whole chapter but that it fits well into a kind of comic lyricism. The expected 'swirling pool' undergoes an easy transposition which quells the danger of cliché. 'Bungholes' colours the whole sentence and mocks the poetry it begets. If the following were in Joyce's pale volume *Chamber Music* we should think little enough of it:

> O let us linger my love by this river of ours,
> Winding through mudflats over the level land,
> A huge dull flood that stretches on hand and hand,
> Bearing along its froth in wideleaved flowers.
> Let us look, my fraillimbed girl,
> On its lazy pooling swirl.

A mark of Joyce's genius was to recognise the smallness of his poetic talent and to see how a fine ear and a weak lyrical impulse could revolutionise the prose of a whole era.

Can (in 8) a smell be cold? Can stone have a smell, especially from a distance? Can stone call? These questions are not to be asked. The sentence is a brief phrase of organ music, with slant-rhymes ('cold' – 'called') enclosing head-rhymes ('sacred' – 'stone'), and 'cold' chiming with 'stone'. And, of course, four of the five key-words have long vowels. In 9 it is the 'keen reek' that gives a brief spasm of pleasure, contrasting as it does with 'dusty dry smell'. One ought not to cavil about whether sponges and loofahs actually possess a smell. Example 10 begins the codetta of the chapter. Bloom is going to have a bath in the mosque-shaped public bathhouse and to masturbate in it (a proposal which his interior monologue is shy of spelling out: 'Also I think I. Yes I. Do it in the bath. Curious longing I.' As in *Finnegans Wake*, semen is confounded with urine: 'Water to water'). His body is to lie in the bath 'at full', as though its pallor were that of the moon. The roundness suggests the host Bloom has just seen elevated in an idle cooling visit to a church; the words immediately preceding this sentence are 'This is my body'. The 'womb of warmth' reshapes the bathtub and sums up the lotus-longing which is really desire for the pre-natal state. The body must be 'laved', not washed, in this ceremony-of-innocence context, with its oil and perfume. 'Naked' floats in parenthesis: *pale naked body* would not do. The melody of the sentence would go well on quiet flutes.

Some of the brief descriptive passages in the 'Wandering Rocks' episode – the last chapter in which prose is used directly and not experimentally or parodically – touch eccentricity but are still brilliantly effective. Again, I take ten examples.

1. A skiff, a crumpled throwaway, Elijah is coming, rode lightly down the Liffey, under Loopline bridge, shooting the rapids where water chafed around the bridgepiers, sailing eastward past hulls and anchorchains, between the Customhouse old dock and George's quay.

2. Two carfuls of tourists passed slowly, their women sitting fore, gripping frankly the handrests.

3. – *Sacrifizio incruento*, Stephen said smiling, swaying his ashplant in slow swingswong from its midpoint, lightly.

4. The vesta in the clergyman's uplifted hand consumed itself in a long soft flame and was let fall. At their feet its red speck died: and mouldy air closed round them.

5. The lacquey, aware of comment, shook the lolling clapper of his bell but feebly.

6. John Howard Parnell translated a white bishop quietly and his grey claw went up again to his forehead whereat it rested.

7. As he strode past Mr Bloom's dental windows the sway of his dustcoat brushed rudely from its angle a slender tapping cane and swept onwards, having buffeted a thewless body. The blind stripling turned his sickly face after the striding form.

8. John Henry Menton, filling the doorway of Commercial Buildings, stared from winebig oyster eyes, holding a fat gold hunter watch not looked at in his fat left hand not feeling it.

9. From its sluice in Wood quay wall under Tom Devan's office Poddle river hung out in fealty a tongue of liquid sewage.
10. From Cahill's corner the reverend Hugh C. Love, M.A., made obeisance unperceived, mindful of lords deputies whose hands benignant had held of yore rich advowsons.

In the first example there is nothing very remarkable about the construction, but there is a certain lightheaded whimsy – appropriate to the time of day, when many Dubliners are drunk and most are temporarily fatigued – in the turning of a throwaway leaflet into a manned skiff.* We do not have to be given the full adjective-group 'on which the legend *Elijah is coming* was inscribed'. The elliptical reference Joyce uses is an agent of aggrandisement (this is only a piece of paper), as is the news, which still lies in the future, of Throwaway's winning the Ascot Gold Cup (the tip was given accidentally by Bloom in the 'Lotus Eaters' chapter and it will prove a cause of hate in the chapter to come). This is a quite straightforward descriptive sentence otherwise, in which the gentle personification (abetted by the 'chafing' of the water) is hardly to be noticed. Sentence 2 is notable for the nautical, or archaic, 'fore' and for the position of 'frankly', which orthodox style would prefer after the object of the verb. 'Frankly' is in itself a surprising word in this context. Normally used to modify statements or acts on which a social judgment may be made, it is here employed in the sense of *openly*, on the fringe of 'in awareness that there was no real need to grip the handrests as a jolting passage was not to be expected, and in mild defiance of onlookers who might consider such a safety measure totally unnecessary'. This postposition is, by the way, conceivably influenced by the dialogue of the section, which is all in Italian – in Italian the arrangement would be normal – but Joyce is ready to displace in this manner without contextual encouragement. Sentence 3, from the same section, has Stephen telling his music-teacher that the sacrifice of his singing voice is a bloodless one (specifically *sacrifizio incruento* designates the Catholic mass) and making the balancing gesture with his ash-plant a symbol of his lack of concern. Singing a song is turned

* Suggesting also the Ship *Argo* which sailed between the 'Floating Rocks' which provide the classical – but non-Homeric – counterpart of the chapter.

into swinging a swong. The final 'lightly' is not in its normal position and is deliberately ambiguous: it can modify both 'said' and 'swaying'.

The match in 4 has become, like the sailing throwaway of 1, a personified agent (how appropriate a vesta is, incidentally, for a clergyman; a match would do for the laity). 'Was let fall' would, I think, be inadmissible in British English, which would prefer *was allowed to fall*, but Joyce may have changed all that. Certainly, as in the 'I done me best when I was let' of *Finnegans Wake*, the usage has an Irish flavour about it. The 'mouldy air', like the vesta, has a life of its own: it performs the act of enclosing. For the sake of brevity, in 5, Joyce is willing to use, as on other occasions, an archaism. 'But feebly' is certainly neater than *again but this time somewhat feebly*. 'Aware of comment' is not quite archaic, but it has a formal quality about it which, in the context, is mildly humorous.

In 6, Parnell's brother is playing chess in the D.B.C. teashop. A real episcopal bishop is translated to another see; to use the term of the moving of a chess bishop on the board is a sort of mild donnish joke, but it is satisfying, as tiny pedantry frequently is. The 'grey claw' has, apparently, a life of its own like the throwaway, vesta and mouldy air; the archaic 'whereat' is neater than *at which* (clumsy) or *on which* (suggestive of an alighting fly). The 'he' of 7 is Cashel Boyle O'Connor Fitzmaurice Tisdall Farrell, a transitory madman. (The dental Bloom is no relative of Leopold.) He is brought in because of the sense of danger of bumping into the wrong thing decreed by the presiding wandering rocks. It is the body of the blind piano-tuner who is the pedal-point of the 'Sirens' fugue which is 'thewless' – again an archaism that works. The 'buffeted' may seem too strong a word for the brushing of a light coat against a human form, but it is justified by those rocks. The transference of 'dental' from Mr Bloom to his windows may hardly be noticed, but by now we have become used to Joyce's technique.

The last three sentences come in the final section of the chapter, when the viceregal cavalcade moves in full observed splendour towards the Mirus bazaar, which the viceroy is to open. There is nothing really exceptional about 8, though it looks eccentric. The economy of putting Menton's presumed luncheon into his eyes is typical Joyce. Menton neither looks at nor feels his watch because he is staring at the passing viceroy and his entourage. Other writers might prefer *at which he did not look, in his fat left hand, which did not feel it* or even *which was not sensible of it*, but Joyce will always avoid a subordinate clause if he can. The personification of 9, along with 'fealty', combines two tendencies of the language in the chapter – to give inanimate things a kind of responsible life, since they, like human beings, are set on a course which must not collide with other courses; to hint at fixed order – symbolised in church and state, which help to prevent collisions in human affairs, and in the ancient stable legal terms which reflect their power to do this. But Joyce would probably have written in no different manner here if this symbolism had not been implied. The reverend Mr Love of 10 is an Anglican clergyman and he floods his brief sentence with proctorial English, or the impersonal animated glossary in Joyce does it for him.

There are two remarkable brief paragraphs in 'Wandering Rocks' which present, in impersonal third-person form, transitory visions of the two main characters. When Bloom at a bookstall is examining a piece of near-pornography called *Sweets of Sin*, he is moved, at the usual preconscious level, by extracts like 'All the dollarbills her husband gave her were spent in the stores on wondrous gowns and costliest frillies. For him! For Raoul!' and 'The beautiful woman threw off her sabletrimmed wrap, displaying her queenly shoulders and heaving embonpoint.' This is the verbal equivalent of what then ensues:

Warmth showered gently over him, cowing his flesh. Flesh yielded amid rumpled clothes. Whites of eyes swooning up. His nostrils arched themselves for prey. Melting breast ointments (*for him*! *For Raoul*!). Armpits' oniony sweat. Fishgluey slime (*her heaving embonpoint*!) Feel! Press! Crushed! Sulphur dung of lions!

Young! Young!

This is very daring, but it is no more than the culmination of the impressionism already noted in calmer renderings of the world outside the consciousness. It is also very funny. In Stephen's vision, rubies seen in a jeweller's window call up an image of 'muddy swinesnouts, hands,' which 'root and root, gripe and wrest them' and then this:

She dances in a foul gloom where gum burns with garlic. A sailorman, rustbearded, sips from a beaker rum and eyes her. A long and seafed silent rut. She dances, capers, wagging her sowish haunches and her hips, on her gross belly flapping a ruby egg.

This seems to me to be an outstanding piece of descriptive prose which, more than anything in the unfantasticated parts of *Ulysses*, exemplifies Joyce's gift for conveying a rich image with great economy. Only one subordinate clause is needed. The adjective 'rustbearded' is suspended in postposition and carries a visual weight it would not have if it preceded its noun and threw the vocal accent on to it. The adverb phrase 'from a beaker' follows its verb and its complex effectiveness can best be gauged by shifting it to the more usual slot. In the verbless sentence that follows an astonishing amount of information is conveyed. The final sentence, with its ambiguous subordinate phrase ('flapping' can be transitive or intransitive), and the sluggishness of movement imposed by the aspirates, palatal fricatives and long vowels and diphthongs, is an exact rendering of the dancer's lascivious clumsiness. The triumph, as nearly always, is a musical one which does not yield easily to analysis.

(I cannot resist mentioning here that in the thoughts that follow – Stephen wresting old images from the earth like rubies; converting the gross belly into a more comely image – Joyce commits for the second time his one sin of anachronism. In 'Proteus' Stephen has thought of Eve's 'belly without blemish, bulging big, a buckler of taut vellum, no, whiteheaped corn, orient and immortal, standing from everlasting to everlasting'. Here again he mentions to himself 'Orient and immortal wheat standing from everlasting to everlasting'. The phrase comes from Thomas Traherne's *Centuries of Meditation*, which was not published until 1908, four years after Bloomsday. One points the finger only because Joyce is otherwise so meticulous in keeping his known future out of his reconstructed past.)

It should be possible, knowing something of Joyce's prose technique, to rewrite as an exercise part of a Class 1 novel in a style approaching his. I take at random a passage from Arthur Hailey's bestselling novel *Hotel* ('Over 3,000,000 copies in print!' cries the cover of the paperback):

'Doctor,' Christine said, 'just this moment . . .'

The newcomer nodded and from a leather bag, which he put down on the bed, swiftly produced a stethoscope. Without wasting time he reached inside the patient's flannel nightshirt and listened briefly to the chest and back. Then, returning to the bag, in a series of efficient movements he took out a syringe, assembled it, and snapped off the neck of a small glass vial. When he had drawn the fluid from the vial into the syringe, he leaned over the bed and pushed a sleeve of the nightshirt upward, twisting it into a rough tourniquet. He instructed Christine, 'Keep that in place; hold it tightly.'

This is one of those utilitarian bridge-passages which all novels must have, and it does not call for fine writing. Nevertheless Joyce might be unable to resist counterpointing with the essential narrative a detached verbal melody and, turning Christine into a female Stephen, a fragment of internal monologue. And – a small point – he would certainly substitute 'said' for 'instructed': 'coloured' verbs of saying fight against detachment.

– Doctor, Christine said, just this moment –

He placed with grace on the bed, nodding, his leather bag and snaked out swiftly a stethoscope. *Hirudo medicinalis*, a leech for a leech. With grace of speed he nuzzled the cold steel snout in under the flannel nightshirt, cocking a perked ear to back and chest and back again. Back at his bag, he assembled a syringe from glass tubes and a glancing needle and smartly cracked the neck of a vial. With care he watched the fluid follow the track of the retracting plunger then, leaning over the bed, pushtwisted up a nightshirtsleeve into a rough tourniquet. He said to Christine:

– Keep that in place. Hold it tight.

Something like that, only much much better.

CHAPTER 6

Musicalisation

ᘓᘓᘓᘓᘓᘓ

THE 'Wandering Rocks' episode is a small labyrinth at the very centre of the huge labyrinth which is *Ulysses*. At three in the afternoon, when the events and non-events of the episode are occurring, we are permitted to take a breathing-spell from the slow diachronic treadmill of narrative and look down on the whole structure for a space. We even move outside the Odyssey, finding our classical parallel in the perilous journey of Jason and the Argonauts, who had to navigate with great care between the clashing Symplegades. There are eighteen sections, corresponding to the eighteen chapters of the whole book, and these sections must be viewed synchronically: Joyce constructed them like an engineer (mechanics is the 'art' of this chapter), with a stopwatch and a map of Dublin in front of him. The synchronic approach is, however, difficult in a diachronic medium like language, and we can only *seem* to make it through trickery. Joyce's trickery consists in interpolating sentences from one section into another, informing us by a quick signal that this event is proceeding simultaneously with that. While Mr Kernan is in James's Street, Mr Dedalus and his daughter are some distance away, near Dillon's auction-rooms. Here is the counterpoint made between them:

– Where would I get money? Mr Dedalus asked. There is no-one in Dublin would lend me fourpence.

– You got some, Dilly said, looking in his eyes.

– How do you know that? Mr Dedalus asked, his tongue in his cheek.

Mr Kernan, pleased with the order he had booked, walked boldly along James's street.

– I know you did, Dilly answered. Were you in the Scotch house now?

Temple Bar is a long way from the Phoenix Park, where the viceroy's procession begins:

While he waited in Temple bar McCoy dodged a banana peel with gentle pushes of his toe from the path to the gutter. Fellow might damn easy get a nasty fall there coming along tight in the dark.*

The gates of the drive opened wide to give egress to the viceregal cavalcade.
– Even money, Lenehan said returning. I knocked against Bantam Lyons in there going to back a bloody horse someone gave him that hasn't an earthly.

Joyce, clicking his stopwatch, notes the simultaneity of Lenehan's words and the opening of the gates of the viceregal lodge.

The trick is essentially a musical one. All writers, especially those who, like Joyce, have had musical training, must envy the ability of the musical composer to work in time and space at the same time (or space). We read from left to right along a musical score and take in a diachronic image; we read from top to bottom and hear in our imagination many contrapuntal lines conceived synchronically. That Dedalus-Kernan or viceroy-Lenehan counterpoint could be more than mere literary trickery in an operatic adaptation with a split stage (or, better, screen), but Joyce is limited to signs on paper. Still, it is appropriate that, challenged by music in the 'Wandering Rocks' chapter, he should seek to meet the challenge in the episode that follows. The mechanical labyrinth is succeeded by a human one, symbolised in the whorls of the ear. Music plays us in – a band of 'highland laddies' discoursing 'My Girl's a Yorkshire Girl' at the tail of the viceregal procession – but the 'Sirens' scene wants more than a popular tune: it seeks to create a fugue of more than Bachian complexity.

The device, which I discussed in the first chapter, of displacing fragments from the episode and placing them at the beginning, to make a kind of prelude to the fugue, is no more than a gigantic augmentation of the 'Wandering Rocks' technique, and it suggests Wagnerian *leitmotiv* (especially as it ends with a reminiscence of one of Walther's trial songs) more than the baroque atmosphere of the fugal form. But it will do for symbolising the broken bones of men rent and devoured by the Sirens. The

* The banana peel is a wandering rock.

Sirens themselves, however, do not seem to be very formidable. They are two barmaids in the Ormond Hotel, cowering 'under their reef of counter' while they drink tea, not blood, preparing for mechanical flirtation with the customers. They seem to be tempting enough, but not devastatingly so. Bloom comes to the Ormond after buying notepaper to write a letter to his penfriend Martha; he eats a meal of liver and bacon in the restaurant (still fond of inner organs, still defiant of ancestral dietary taboos). He drinks cider which, combining with the lunchtime burgundy, makes his own coda play an eventual coda to the fugue: there human language breaks down, but first it has to be exalted into a diviner art. The chapter is full of song coming from the music-room, where the piano has just been tuned, and of Bloom's own meditations on music, and these do more to remind us of the Homeric parallel than the deeper structure can. It turns out that the Sirens themselves represent the fugal subject – the theme on which the whole fugue is based – and that Bloom represents the answer, which is technically the subject re-stated in another voice, a fifth higher or a fourth lower. Blazes Boylan, who is on his way to commit adultery with Bloom's wife, stands for the counter-subject – the contrapuntal accompaniment to the answer and, from then on, to every re-statement of the subject. If Joyce had been really pedantic in this chapter, he could have made the names of the sirens contain enough musical notes for a lengthy phrase, but he contents himself with calling Miss Kennedy Mina (minor) and Miss Douce Lydia (a reference to the Lydian scale – F major with a B natural, not a B flat). The musical letters in their combined full names give us A E E D D A D C E, which, expressed in an appropriate rhythm, spell out the following theme:

Bloom's answer should then properly consist of the notes E A A A A E A G B, but it is not possible to find them all in the three names he may be said to have: Virag (his original Hungarian name), Henry Flower (the pseudonym he uses for writing to Martha Clifford), and the name Dublin and the world know best. Joyce does not go so far, though I cannot help thinking that he makes Bloom drink cider because CIDER contains the first three notes of the scale of C major.

There are the usual 'episodes' between the fugal re-entries, and these are mostly provided by Mr Dedalus, tenor, and Ben Dollard, bass. Only one of the Sirens sings – Miss Douce – and she does not know the words of her song very well – 'O Idolores, queen of the eastern seas', meaning '*my* Dolores'. As the fugue moves to its end, the tap of the stick of the piano-tuner – the 'blind stripling' we have already met briefly – provides a pedal-point – 'Tap. Tap. Tap.' (Compare the oft-repeated 'Tip' of *Finnegans Wake*.) The young man has left his tuning-fork on the piano he has tuned, and he comes back for it, making the approaching tap of his stick symbolise the fixed and unchanging note of the fork itself, holding all the divergent strands of counter-point together. Here is an early part of the fugue:

Gaily Miss Douce polished a tumbler, trilling:

– *O Idolores, queen of the eastern seas*!
– Was Mr Lidwell in today?

In came Lenehan. Round him peered Lenehan. Mr Bloom reached Essex bridge. Yes, Mr Bloom crossed bridge of Yessex. To Martha I must write. Buy paper. Daly's. Girl there civil. Bloom. Old Bloom. Blue Bloom is on the rye.

– He was in at lunchtime, Miss Douce said.

Lenehan came forward.

– Was Mr Boylan looking for me?

He asked. She answered:

– Miss Kennedy, was Mr Boylan in while I was upstairs?

She asked. Miss voice of Kennedy answered, a second teacup poised, her gaze upon a page.

– No. He was not.

Miss gaze of Kennedy, heard not seen, read on. Lenehan round the sandwichbell wound his round body round.

– Peep! Who's in the corner?

No glance of Kennedy rewarding him he yet made overtures. To mind her stops. To read only the black ones: round o and crooked ess.

Jingle jaunty jingle.

Miss Douce and Miss Kennedy, together or singly, vocally or silently, give out the fugue-subject. The narrative moves on, with the entry (not a fugal entry) of Lenehan. Bloom, though more than an interval of five or four full tones away, sounds the

expected answer, and a reference to Boylan provides the counter-
subject. The passage is full of musical references – the song 'The
Bloom is on the Rye', Lenehan's 'overtures', Miss Kennedy's
'stops', the 'bell' that holds the sandwiches – as well as a franker
use of sound-play than Joyce has so far allowed himself ('wound
his round body round'), some of which imitates musical technique: 'Mr Bloom reached Essex bridge. Yes, Mr Bloom crossed
bridge of Yessex' – a varied repetition, with – 'yes', 'Yessex' –
imitation. The dialogue suggests recitative, the 'He asked' and
'She asked' obviously mimicking the conventional cadences that
we associate with it. Joyce also prepares a very economical way
of making the fugal voices sing, or be imagined as singing. The
'Jingle jaunty jingle', a detached nonsensical offering at the end,
makes all too much sense. Boylan is coming in a jauntily jingling
cab, and he will soon be proceeding to Mr Bloom's residence,
where the bed is old and the springs, especially when strongly
agitated, jingle too. If there is prolepsis, there is also reminiscence: the presence of Lenehan in the bar makes Bloom become
the 'old Bloom' who, said Lenehan in the previous chapter, has
'a touch of the artist' about him. Generally, then, Joyce takes
expected advantage of the musical ambient to sound his vowels,
play tricks with his syntax, and bring the texture of words closer
to that of their sisters, notes, than he has dared in sterner contexts.

When song, or the instruments of song, have to be described,
then we know that Joyce will move from the contrapuntal to the
lyrical:

A duodene of birdnotes chirruped bright treble answer under sensitive
hands. Brightly the keys, all twinkling, linked, all harpsichording,
called to a voice to sing the strain of dewy morn, of youth, of love's
leavetaking, life's, love's morn.

The piano seems to play itself a Beethoven sonata, complete with
sudden chordal surprises:

Upholding the lid he (who?) gazed in the coffin (coffin?) at the oblique
triple (piano!) wires. He pressed (the same who pressed indulgently
her hand), soft pedalling a triple of keys to see the thicknesses of felt
advancing, to hear the muffled hammerfall in action.

This decorative kind of writing can serve, in terms of the essential fictional purpose of the book, to do more than tutting ortho-

doxy might believe possible. It is musically apposite that Boylan should ask one of the barmaids to snap her garter for him – '*Sonnez la cloche*'. Also that Lenehan, who describes Blazes as 'Boyland with impatience', should ask him irritably 'Got the horn or what?' But these little themes combine to make a tune that characterises this Dublin Don Giovanni perfectly:

By Bachelor's walk jogjaunty jingled Blazes Boylan, bachelor, in sun, in heat, mare's glossy rump atrot, with flick of whip, on bounding tyres: sprawled, warmseated, Boylan impatience, ardentbold. Horn. Have you the? Horn. Have you the? Horn. Have you the? Haw haw horn.

He moves on towards Eccles Street:

Jingle by monuments of Sir John Gray, Horatio onehandled Nelson, reverend father Theobald Matthew, jaunted as said before just now. Atrot, in heat, heatseated. *Cloche*. *Sonnez la*. *Cloche*. *Sonnez la*. Slower the mare went up the hill by the Rotunda, Rutland square. Too slow for Boylan, blazes Boylan, impatience Boylan, joggled the mare.

Soon he is near Bloom's kidneyseller. As the tmetic epithet for Nelson above derives from Stephen's story about the old ladies who visit Nelson's pillar – 'the onehandled adulterer' – so what comes now borrows from Bloom's morning vision of bright-tubed sausages and his reading of the 'Agendath Netaim' advertisement in the butcher's where he bought his kidney:

This is the jingle that joggled and jingled. By Dlugacz's porkshop bright tubes of Agendath trotted a gallantbuttocked mare.

While Bloom, liver and bacon finished, is writing his letter to Martha (who is inevitably celebrated in song by Mr Dedalus – *M'appari*, from the opera *Martha*), Boylan arrives at No. 7 Eccles Street:

Jog jig jogged stopped. Dandy tan shoe of dandy Boylan socks skyblue clocks came light to earth.

We have met those socks and shoes in the preceding chapter. Now music is debased through Boylan's lust into crass animal rhythms:

One rapped on a door, one tapped with a knock, did he knock Paul de Kock, with a loud proud knocker, with a cock carracarracarra cock. Cockcock.

Boylan has already been identified – for future phantasmagoric purposes – with the Raoul of *Sweets of Sin*. Now he becomes the actual writer of certain spicy romances beloved of Molly Bloom ('Paul de Kock. Nice name he has.') It is Boylan who initiates the reduction of the noble fugal structure to mere noise. Bloom's bodily discomfort with the cider or 'the bur' produces borborygms, glasses clink 'Tschink. Tschunk.', the stripling's stick taps, a tram goes 'Kran, kran, kran', and only the words of Robert Emmet, which Bloom reads in a shop window, make either prosodic or semantic sense. But their import is, in effect, to be debased – through association with stupid chauvinism – in the chapter that follows.

Joyce takes the musicalisation of his prose even further in the 'Circe' episode than in the 'Sirens' fugue. 'Circe' is presented in dramatic form, and Joyce has to find a style for his stage-directions which exemplifies the two presiding themes – animality and magic (men are turned into more than swine in Nighttown). It is appropriate that this kind of thing should happen when a dance strikes up in Bella Cohen's house ('not a brothel,' she says):

(*He wheels Kitty into Lynch's arms, snatches up his ashplant from the table and takes the floor. All wheel, whirl, waltz, twirl. Bloombella, Kittylynch, Florryzoe, jujuby women. Stephen with hat ashplant frogsplits in middle highkicks with skykicking mouth shut hand clasp part under thigh, with clang tinkle boomhammer tallyho hornblower blue green yellow flashes. Toft's cumbersome turns with hobbyhorse riders from gilded snakes dangled, bowels fandango leaping spurn soil foot and fall again.*)

The pianola plays 'My Girl's a Yorkshire Girl', and both the tune and the whirl of the dance are rendered in a surrealistic-seeming style which picks fragments from various of the past chapters. Let us examine some of the fragments before we see them swirl together.

In the 'Wandering Rocks' episode Dilly Dedalus, Stephen's sister, sees and hears the 'lacquey by the door of Dillon's auction-rooms' shake his handbell: 'Barang!' then 'Bang!' then, after a feeble shaking in response to Mr Dedalus's curse, a loud bang again. In the same episode, a one-legged sailor swings his way from Eccles Street, singing, receiving an alms from Molly Bloom. Corny Kelleher, the undertaker, at the same time 'closed his long daybook and glanced with his drooping eye at a pine coffinlid sentried in a corner'. In the 'AEolus' chapter Stephen told the story of the two '*Frauenzimmer*' (so named in 'Proteus') who climbed to the top of the 'onehandled adulterer's' column and spat down plumstones. Bloom, nearing the beginning of his Odyssey, saw the poster of a cycle race showing a 'cyclist doubled up like a cod in a pot'. In the 'Cyclops' scene the Provost-marshal wept over the beauty of the girl of a man due for hanging: 'Blimey it makes me kind of bleeding cry, straight it does, when I see her cause I thinks of my old mashtub what's waiting for me down Limehouse way.' Add Father Conmee, the Reverend Love, Stephen's 'Proteus' memory of exiled Kevin Egan's lighting a 'gunpowder' cigarette with 'a blue fuse match', odd beast-themes, drum-beats, and the words of 'My Girl's a Yorkshire Girl', and we end up with the following:

(*Bang fresh barang bang of lacquey's bell, horse, nag, steer, piglings, Conmee on Christass lame crutch and leg sailor in cockboat armfolded ropepulling hitching stamp hornpipe through and through, Baraabum! On nags, hogs, bellhorses, Gadarene swine, Corny in coffin. Steel shark stone onehandled Nelson, two trickies Frauenzimmer plumstained from pram falling bawling. Gum, he's a champion. Fuseblue peer from barrel rev. evensong Love on hackney jaunt Blazes blind coddoubled bicyclers Dilly with snowcake no fancy clothes. then in last wiswitchback lumbering up and down bump mashtup sort of viceroy and reine relish for tublumber bumpshire rose. Baraabum!*)

This may be regarded as one step up from gibberish, despite its provenance in narrative sense; but in a scene where men are set upon by sorcery and reduced to slobbering beasts, any fracturing of language is in order. Yet Joyce prefers to justify his fracturing in musical rather than mimetic terms. In a closely organised musical piece, like the first movement of a classical sonata or symphony, no theme may be presented in the expository section unless it is repeated – for purposes of pure balance – in the recapitulation. Between these two parts of the movement lies the free fantasia or development section, and here the composer will show the plastic potentiality of themes already presented – combining them, exaggerating their rhythmic or tonal features, shifting them from key to key. 'Circe' may be taken as the development section of the symphonic structure which is *Ulysses*, and here the breakdown of time, space and probability encourages Joyce to treat plastically material drawn from earlier chapters. It is doubtful if even the most trivial *donnée* of the naturalistic episodes is neglected. Nor does Joyce confine this technique solely to 'Circe'. We have already seen how the 'Agendath Netaim' advertisement of Bloom's butcher's wrapping sheets has been drawn into Boylan's silly jingle. In the 'Oxen of the Sun' chapter, as we shall see soon, Joyce uses any scrap of past material that offers as theme for a mode of writing that calls attention to texture more than content. If one has had any experience at all of musical composition, one will fancy that in Joyce, as he approached the nocturnal part of his book, there was a kind of composer's disquiet at having fired so many themes at his audience without making these themes justify themselves in formal terms, as opposed to the demands of naturalistic narrative. Hence the free fantasias of the night, where what often looks like nonsense is really music.

Joyce recognised, more than any literary artist of our century, the close kinship between music and poetry (or Class 2 fiction). Both literature and music are realised through time, but music has an apparent spatial dimension as well, except when it is pure monody. There is counterpoint, which Joyce imitates but never with a satisfying exactness, and there is also harmony. We can strike a word on the typewriter, but on the piano we can strike a chord, and a chord is more than a compound of sounded notes: it is also a complex of harmonics. Traditional literature at its greatest could make a single word a rich experience ('incarnadine' and '*rooky* wood' in *Macbeth*, for instance), but, as music needed Debussy to realise harmonics as explicit parts of a chord, so literature has needed to learn how to exploit all the connotations that lie latent in a word. If verbal richness had, in the past, been achieved by instinct, one of the aims of modern writing must be to make its attainment a conscious process.

Of all writers in English, two have seemed to seek verbal denseness through an envy of the resources of music. One, of course, is Joyce, and the other is Gerard Manley Hopkins. Hopkins died seven years after Joyce was born, but the fact that Hopkins, a convert to Catholicism and a Jesuit priest, taught at University College, Dublin, where Joyce was eventually a student, has led some readers of both, careless about chronology, to assume that Hopkins influenced Joyce. Even W. H. Gardner, a great Hopkins scholar, has said: '. . . it is likely that James

Joyce, E. E. Cummings and Dylan Thomas were decisively affected by a reading of Hopkins.' One might note in passing that the influence on Cummings was minimal, that Thomas scrupulously turned his ear against sprung rhythm, and then demonstrate, from dates, that Joyce's mature style was formed before Hopkins's collected volume was published – posthumously in 1918. There is one passage in *Finnegans Wake* that seems deliberately to evoke Hopkins – the description of the sleeping Isobel towards the end – but all the rest is coincidence. The coincidence is close. Both men pursued the same end out of the same temperament. Both made aesthetic philosophies out of the schoolmen – Joyce from Aquinas, Hopkins from Duns Scotus. Joyce saw 'epiphanies' flashing out of the current of everyday life; Hopkins observed nature and felt the 'instress' of 'inscapes'.

Both were equally obsessed with language and equally knowledgeable about music. (Hopkins's song 'Falling Rain' uses quartertones long before the experimental Central Europeans and even anticipates the notation now used in microtonal writing.) Make a context question out of mixed fragments, and you will sometimes find it hard to tell one author from the other. 'Forwardlike, but however, and like favourable heaven heard these' might do for a Stephen Dedalus interior monologue; actually it comes from 'The Bugler's First Communion'; 'Muddy swinesnouts, hands, root and root, gripe and wrest them' is from 'Wandering Rocks' but would do for a Hopkins poem about martyrs. The eschewal of hyphens helps the resemblance: 'fallowbootfellow' is from the sonnet 'Tom's Garland' but it will do for both. The kinship goes deeper than compressed syntax, a love of compound words, and a devotion to Anglo-Saxonisms. They were both concerned with bringing literature closer to music.

Hopkins was primarily a poet, whereas poetry to Joyce became a side-art, and Hopkins's innovation, sprung rhythm, which brought to verse the freedom of the musical flow, finds no parallel in Joyce, whose prose has all the freedom it needs, as well as the intensity tradition associates with poetry. But in Joyce we find the same *sforzandi* as in Hopkins, signalled by heavy headrhymes. ('Part, pen, pack' is typical Hopkins, meaning 'separate the sheep from the goats, pen the sheep and send the goats packing'.) We find also the same internal rhymes (as in Hopkins's 'each

tucked string tells, each hung bell's / Bow swung finds tongue to
fling out broad its name'), so that we seem to be listening to the
effects of repetition-with-a-difference that are the essence of
musical phrases. But, most important resemblance of all, every
statement in both must have the solidity of content of a sequence
of chords, or else the sense of multiple significance we find in
polyphony. There is no space for the purely functional, since in
music nothing is purely functional.

Hence that compression in both that sometimes causes difficulties. Here is Hopkins, and again it might be Joyce: 'the utter-
most mark / Our passionplunged giant risen' or 'rare gold, bold
steel, bare / In both; dare but share care . . .' or 'that treads
through, prickproof, thick / Thousands of thorns, thoughts'.
In striving to catch a single meaning, we catch more than one;
sometimes in Hopkins – as with 'thorns, thoughts' – two words
seem to merge into each other, becoming a new word, and what
one might call an auditory iridescence gives a powerful contrapuntal effect. Joyce, living later than Hopkins, was able to go
further, blending words boldly into genuine chords. The words
of *Finnegans Wake* are nearly all chords. Instead of merely juxta-
posing *thorns* and *thoughts*, as Hopkins had to do, Joyce was able,
if he wished, to combine them into '*thornghts*'. A typical *Finnegans
Wake* chord is 'crossmess parzle' – descriptive of life, as of the
book itself: a fusion of *crossword puzzle* and *Christmas parcel*. But
we must defer our discussion of the music of that difficult work
until we have considered why Joyce wrote the work in the first
place. It is enough for now to recognise that, with him, musicalisation is never a matter of mere decorative fancy. If literature, as
it should, ever learns to ransack its sister art's resources to the
end of its own legitimate aggrandisement, it will not be works like
Aldous Huxley's *Point Counter Point* or T. S. Eliot's *Four Quartets*
that will have shown the way (these touch music only with the
fingernail): it will be, as in so many other literary advances,
Ulysses.

CHAPTER 7

Borrowed Styles

🙰🙰🙰🙰🙰🙰

FROM the 'Cyclops' chapter on, one becomes aware that Joyce
has changed his stylistic approach to *Ulysses* in two modes: the
sections become longer, as though the time needed for reading
them must now match exactly the time taken for the enactment
of the events described; and there is an enormously increased
use of pastiche or parody. These two terms cause difficulty when
applied to Joyce. Properly, a pastiche is an imitation of an existing
artistic style, so close and skilful as to be indistinguishable from
the original. A parody is also an imitation, but one that so
exaggerates the characteristics of the original as to provoke various
kinds of laughter, from the affectionate to the scornful. There are
specimens in *Ulysses* of undoubted parody, like this from Buck
Mulligan, which ridicules the new Irish drama:

– It's what I'm telling you, mister honey, it's queer and sick we were,
Haines and myself, the time himself brought it in. 'Twas murmur we
did for a gallus potion would rouse a friar, I'm thinking, and he limp
with leching. And we one hour and two hours and three hours in
Connery's sitting civil waiting for pints apiece.

In 'Circe', the same style is briefly imposed on Bloom, who
appears 'in caubeen with clay pipe stuck in the band, dusty
brogues, an emigrant's red handkerchief bundle in his hand,
leading a black bogoak pig by a sugaun, with a smile in his eye'
and is made to say:

Let me be going now, woman of the house, for by all the goats in
Connemara I'm after having the father and mother of a bating.

'Circe' is rich in apparent mockeries of various kinds of English,
like this speech made by the ghost of Bloom's grandfather,
Virag:

Lyum! Look. Her beam is broad. She is coated with quite a considerable layer of fat. Obviously mammal in weight of bosom you remark that she has in front well to the fore two protuberances of very respectable dimensions, inclined to fall in the noonday soupplate, while on her rere lower down are two additional protuberances, suggestive of potent rectum and tumescent for palpation which leave nothing to be desired save compactness. Such fleshy parts are the product of careful nurture.

But it is difficult here to decide what precisely is being parodied – the style of a foreign professor of art or physiology or gynaecology or the breeding of domestic fowl? As so often, the joke is subtle, deriving from the incompatibility of elements within a given idiolect, and the incompatibility of the subject described with the mode of speech used to describe it. Also in 'Circe', Stephen Dedalus is turned into a brothel tout:

Thousand places of entertainment to expenses your evenings with lovely ladies saling gloves and other things perhaps her heart beerchops perfect fashionable house very eccentric where lots cocottes beautiful dressed much about princesses like are dancing cancan and walking there parisian clowneries extra foolish for bachelors foreigns the same if talking a poor english how much smart they are on things love and sensations voluptuous.

And so on, at great length. Is it the French language itself that is being made to sound ridiculous through literal transference of its accidence and syntax as well as lexis, or is it a low French barker speaking his own brand of English? The real bizarre humour resides in the incompatibility of the role imposed on Stephen – who 'gobbles, with marionette jerks' – with his rarefied poetic true nature.

The long stretches of borrowed style which we find in 'Cyclops' the total takeover of woman's magazine style in 'Nausicaa' and of provincial journalese in 'Eumaeus' are obviously a very different matter from the odd flashes of mockery in other chapters. Joyce is looking for new modes of narration which shall not only be appropriate to subject-matter as well as Homeric correspondence but shall fulfil his need to remove himself entirely from the narration. Towards the end of 'Sirens' he must have recognised that he had come close to revealing himself, even in the mere act of collating Stephen's 'onehandled adulterer' and Bloom's morning kidney in the music that jogs Boylan to Eccles

Street. In 'Circe' he seems to reveal himself too, in the stage directions, but we can imagine there that some malign force – the devil of the magic of which Circe is an agent – has taken possession of the drama, rendering the author himself helpless to interfere. It is more difficult, in 'Sirens', to think of St Cecilia as being in charge: it sounds very much like Joyce at the piano. To hand the narration over to the nameless cadger of 'Cyclops', and also to intermittent impersonal styles, is a way out of the problem of presenting Bloom as a genuine hero in a giant's cave without seeming to introduce value-judgments of the author's own. In all the subsequent chapters total objectivity is achieved through the borrowing of styles. Parody is not the point; indeed, parody implies too much of a critical attitude on the part of the author. The success or otherwise of pastiche, however, is highly relevant, since the failure of the author to achieve an exact likeness will let the author into the narrative, through some hole or other in a badly woven texture. Above everything, the creator must be completely removed from his creation.

Joyce described the style of 'Cyclops' as gigantism – the blowing up of attitudes into postures too heroic to be true. The heroism is shoddy and so makes itself ridiculous, or else it is shortwinded and soon collapses. The Polyphemus of the chapter is a hard-drinking Irish patriot called the Citizen. He despises Bloom as an uxorious, unmanly, deceitful, contriving Jew and, abetted by other patriots, throws a biscuit-tin at him. The scene is Barney Kiernan's, a pub which, unlike Davy Byrne's, is no longer in existence. It is already part of Irish myth, though not so remote as the myth evoked by Joyce in his epic pastiche:

In Inisfail there lies a land, the land of holy Michan. There rises a watchtower beheld of men afar. There sleep the mighty dead as in life they slept, warriors and princes of high renown. A pleasant land it is in sooth of murmuring waters, fishful streams where sport the gunnard, the plaice, the roach, the halibut, the gibbed haddock, the grilse, the dab, the brill, the flounder, the mixed coarse fish generally and other denizens of the aqueous kingdom too numerous to be enumerated.

The gigantesque style can encompass factual lies, stale poetic diction, verbal ineptitude, as well as juxtapositions of genuinely heroic language and journalese. Catalogues, conducive of a sense of amplitude and richness, but also of empty display, are essential to the style. These catalogues are indebted to Rabelais. The verbal structures are weak within, but their collapse is often effected through the sudden cutting in of the low colloquial of the narrator:

... and from the gentle declivities of the place of the race of Kiar, their udders distended with superabundance of milk and butts of butter and rennets of cheese and farmer's firkins and targets of lambs and crannocks of corn and oblong eggs, in great hundreds, various in size, the agate with the dun.

So we turned into Barney Kiernan's and there sure enough was the citizen up in the corner having a great confab with himself and that bloody mangy mongrel Garryowen, and he waiting for what the sky would drop in the way of drink.

The citizen himself (to use Joyce's lower case, itself a kind of deflation) is described in properly gigantic terms:

The figure seated on a large boulder at the foot of a round tower was that of a broadshouldered deepchested stronglimbed frankeyed redhaired freely freckled shaggybearded widemouthed largenosed longheaded deepvoiced barekneed brawnyhanded hairylegged ruddyfaced sinewyarmed hero.

From his girdle hang stones on which are 'graven with rude yet striking art the tribal images of many Irish heroes and heroines of antiquity', beginning genuinely with Cuchulin, Conn of hundred battles, Niall of nine hostages and Brian of Kincora but soon taking in Dante Alighieri, the last of the Mohicans, The Man that Broke the Bank at Monte Carlo, Sir Thomas Lipton, The Bold Soldier Boy, Patrick W. Shakespeare, and many other figures of Irish fame. It is not all self-indulgent fancy. In the scene in the National Library, it is speculated whether Hamlet may be an Irishman, since he swears by St Patrick. In the 'Circe' climax, just before Stephen is struck down by a British redcoat, he uses the expression 'The bold soldier boy'. One of Joyce's aims in the book is to demonstrate points of affinity between Stephen and Bloom, in order to justify their mystical father-son relationship. This aim may be seen in the Nelson-Agendath collation of Boylan's music, though it obtrudes overmuch. The connecting links between the two are usually remote and fragile, just as their eventual meeting and colloquy fail to reveal any essential points of contact. It may be said that these points are essentially literary:

Stephen, grown into the mature Joyce, will write a book on Bloom: when – in the Circean fantasy – both Bloom and Stephen look in a mirror they see the face of Shakespeare, as though only a major artist can truly reconcile them. In this 'Cyclops' chapter the ligatures are so thin as not to be noticed.

The epic tone is invoked again and again in the service of trivial actions – like the drawing of beer for Alf Bergan by the bar-curate, 'chivalrous Terence' – and the effect is sometimes more touching than devastating. After all, in a book which seeks to elevate a Jewish advertising broker to Homeric heights, harmless characters may catch some of the brightness. When Bergan swears that he has seen Dignam in the street, though, as Hynes says, 'They took the liberty of burying him this morning', the style changes to that of a report of a society for psychical research; with a touch of the theosophical language associated with Madam Blavatsky's disciples, who included Yeats and AE:

Interrogated as to whether life there resembled our experience in the flesh he stated that he had heard from more favoured beings now in the spirit that their abodes were equipped with every modern home comfort such as tālāfānā, ālāvātār, hātākāldā, wātāklāsāt and that the highest adepts were steeped in waves of volupcy of the very purest nature.

Technical language of a sublunary kind celebrates Bloom's explanation of why a hanged man's penis becomes engorged:

The distinguished scientist Herr Professor Luitpold Blumenduft tendered medical evidence to the effect that the instantaneous fracture of the cervical vertebrae and consequent scission of the spinal cord would, according to the best approved traditions of medical science, be calculated to inevitably produce in the human subject a violent ganglionic stimulus of the nerve centres, causing the pores of the *corpora cavernosa* to rapidly dilate in such a way as to instantaneously facilitate the flow of blood to that part of the human anatomy known as the penis or male organ . . .

Bloom, the hero, seems to come in for a share of mockery here, as well as the debased quality of much technical English (three split infinitives, appropriate in a chapter evoking Homeric violence), but his first name – as Luitpold – reminds us that he is a bold man of the people, and his new second name makes him smell like a rose. Soon Joyce comes to his favourite borrowed style, that of provincial journalism, in the account of a public execution which is also a public holiday:

Special quick excursion trains and upholstered charabancs had been provided for the comfort of our country cousins of whom there were large contingents. Considerable amusement was caused by the favourite Dublin streetsingers L-n-h-n and M-ll-g-n who sang *The Night before Larry was stretched* in their usual mirthprovoking fashion. Our two inimitable drolls did a roaring trade with their broadsheets among lovers of the comedy element and nobody who has a corner in his heart for real Irish fun without vulgarity will grudge them their hardearned pennies.

Note that the two comics are the clowns of the book, Lenehan and Mulligan. The 'Irish fun' seems to be a conscious reminiscence of lines written by Joyce in his youth, when he reviled his fellow-countrymen who 'in a spirit of Irish fun / Killed their leaders one by one'. The ferial execution is appropriate to a chapter in which Irish vindictiveness and sentimentality are celebrated, and the bloated whimsical journalese fits. When the citizen talks to his dog in Irish, this is a pretext for a report in a mixed style – part newspaper, part learned journal:

All those who are interested in the spread of human culture among the lower animals (and their name is legion) should make a point of not missing the really marvellous exhibition of cynanthropy given by the famous old red wolfdog setter formerly known by the *sobriquet* of Garryowen and recently rechristened by his large circle of friends and acquaintances Owen Garry.

Garryowen, or Owen Garry, has uttered a poem which has been translated into English:

The metrical system of the canine original, which recalls the intricate alliterative and isosyllabic rules of the Welsh englyn, is infinitely more complicated but we believe our readers will agree that the spirit has been well caught.

The poem goes:

> The curse of my curse
> Seven days every day
> And seven dry Thursdays
> On you, Barney Kiernan,
> Has no sup of water
> To cool my courage,
> And my guts red roaring
> After Lowry's lights.

This seems to be a very fair example of an Irish rann. It is followed at once by:

So he told Terry to bring some water for the dog and, gob, you could hear him lapping it up a mile off.

Joyce then moves to hyperbolic ancient courtesy:

– Let me, said he, so far presume upon our acquaintance which, however slight it may appear if judged by the standards of mere time, is founded, as I hope and believe, on a sentiment of mutual esteem, as to request of you this favour. But should I have overstepped the limits of reserve let the sincerity of my feelings be the excuse for my boldness . . .

followed shortly afterwards by – prompted by the words of the narrator about Bloom: 'Gob, he'd have a soft hand under a hen' – a patch of infantilism which is not quite speech, not quite writing, not quite English:

Ga Ga Gara. Klook. Klook. Klook. Black Liz is our hen. She lays eggs for us. When she lays her egg she is so glad. Gara. Klook Klook Klook. Then comes good uncle Leo. He puts his hand under black Liz and takes her fresh egg. Ga ga ga ga Gara. Klook Klook Klook.

Then we are into Hansard:

Mr Allfours (Tamoshant. Con.): Honourable members are already in possession of the evidence produced before a committee of the whole house. I feel I cannot usefully add anything to that. The answer to the honourable member's question is in the affirmative.

Then, Irish games having been mentioned, we are back to local journalism and a report on an imaginary meeting:

After an instructive discourse by the chairman, a magnificent oration eloquently and forcibly expressed, a most interesting and instructive discussion of the usual high standard of excellence ensued as to the desirability of the revivability of the ancient games and sports of our ancient panceltic forefathers.

Bloom suggests love as a panacea for the world's troubles, and at once the following breaks out:

Love loves to love love. Nurse loves the new chemist. Constable 14A loves Mary Kelly. Gerty MacDowell loves the boy that has the bicycle. M.B. loves a fair gentleman. Li Chi Han lovey up kissy Cha Pu Chow. Jumbo, the elephant, loves Alice, the elephant. Old Mr Verschoyle with the ear trumpet loves old Mrs Verschoyle with the turnedin eye. The man in the brown macintosh loves a lady who is dead. His Majesty the King loves her Majesty the Queen . . .

Joyce has sprinkled a few narrative references in here. Gerty MacDowell does indeed love a boy with a bicycle, but she gives herself, as an object of onanism, to Bloom in the following chapter. M.B. is Bloom's wife and the fair gentleman is already with her. The man in the brown macintosh appeared earlier today in Glasnevin cemetery, and at last we know what he was doing there. This obliquity of presentation is very Joycean.

These, then, are samples of the styles Joyce employs to interrupt the narrative of his 'Cyclops' chapter – heroic, technical, committee-minute, above all journalese. When the biscuit-tin is eventually thrown at Bloom we are treated to a description of an earthquake:

The catastrophe was terrific and instantaneous in its effect. The observatory of Dunsink registered in all eleven shocks, all of the fifth grade of Mercalli's scale, and there is no record extant of a similar seismic disturbance in our land since the earthquake of 1534, the year of the rebellion of Silken Thomas. The epicentre appears to have been that part of the metropolis which constitutes the Inn's Quay ward and parish of Saint Michan covering a surface of fortyone acres, two roods and one square pole or perch.

But it is the language of the Apocalypse which is reserved for Bloom's escape from the citizen's wrath:

When, lo, there came about them all a great brightness and they beheld the chariot wherein He stood ascend to heaven. And they beheld Him in the chariot, clothed upon in the glory of the brightness, having raiment of the sun, fair as the moon and terrible that for awe they durst not look upon Him. And there came a voice out of heaven, calling: *Elijah! Elijah!* And he answered with a main cry: *Abba! Adonai!* And they beheld Him even Him, ben Bloom Elijah, amid clouds of angels ascend to the glory of the brightness at an angle of fortyfive degrees over Donohoe's in Little Green Street like a shot off a shovel.

We are brought back to earth, though, very rapidly – in a single sentence from biblical to technically descriptive to colloquial.

What emerges from a brilliant and extremely funny set of pastiches or parodies or pastiche-parodies is a sense of the values that the public world tries to impose on the individual – false values which accept patriotism but reject love, exalt the high-sounding over the reasonable, ultimately debase life by debasing language. Joyce gives us specimens of all kinds of puffed-up language, from provincial newspaper reportage to Wardour Street English, taking in also technical jargon, monstrous but vacuous catalogues, rituals from which the life has gone, and the sesquipedalian evasiveness of parliamentary answers. It is the language which the State uses to hide behind when aware of the corruption of its enactments (the pseudo-art presiding here is politics); it is also the language of romanticism gone bad and turned to sentimentality – pretending to feeling when feeling has fled; it is the postures of little men pretending to be big. The communication media inflate language because they dare not be honest and call a spade a spade; popular historical novels falsify the past and simplify the motives of historical change. Bloom blinds the Cyclops not with a burning stake (his 'knockmedown cigar' is an ornament not a weapon) but with truth: he says that Christ was a Jew, which, more than anything, enrages the citizen. But the latter is already chauvinistically blind, and his own language is the language of blindness:

– We'll put force against force, says the citizen. We have our greater Ireland beyond the sea. They were driven out of house and home in the black 47. Their mudcabins and their shielings by the roadside were laid low by the batteringram and the *Times* rubbed its hands and told the whitelivered Saxons there would soon be as few Irish in Ireland as redskins in America. Even the grand Turk sent us his piastres. But the Sassenach tried to starve the nation at home while the land was full of crops that the British hyenas bought and sold in Rio de Janeiro. Ay, they drove out the peasants in hordes. Twenty thousand of them died in the coffinships. But those that came to the land of the free remember the land of bondage. And they will come again and with a vengeance, no cravens, the sons of Granuaile, the champions of Kathleen ni Houlihan.
   – Perfectly true, says Bloom. But my point was . . .

The citizen is no mean orator, but he does not much care about the truth. Bloom stands for fact and verification of fact, as well as for love as a practical measure, not an abstraction (he is only in this den of the citizen because he is trying to help Dignam's widow and children). Reviled because of his use of words like *phenomenon* and *mortgagee*, he at least uses the words correctly: he is not on the side of the windbags. Low as the garrulous narrator is, we can still see him as a creature not easily taken in by humbug and, perhaps, ultimately more favourable to Bloom than he thinks he is. For the citizen he has no liking. His own speech is all deflation.

The style of 'Nausicaa' is cliché-ridden and euphemistic rather than inflated – in other words, it is the style of a woman's magazine of the Edwardian period, specifically an Irish woman's magazine, since it is religiose and almost lachrymosely Marian:

The summer evening had begun to fold the world in its mysterious embrace. Far away in the west the sun was setting and the last glow of all too fleeting day lingered lovingly on sea and strand, on the proud promontory of dear old Howth guarding as ever the waters of the bay, on the weedgrown rocks along Sandymount shore and, last but not least, on the quiet church whence there streamed forth at times upon the stillness the voice of prayer to her who is in her pure radiance a beacon ever to the stormtossed heart of man, Mary, star of the sea.

The style of 'Eumaeus' is its male counterpart:

Preparatory to anything else Mr Bloom brushed off the greater bulk of the shavings and handed Stephen the hat and ashplant and bucked him up generally in orthodox Samaritan fashion, which he very badly needed. His (Stephen's) mind was not exactly what you would call wandering but a bit unsteady and on his expressed desire for some beverage to drink Mr Bloom, in view of the hour it was and there being no pumps of Vartry water available for their ablutions, let alone drinking purposes, hit upon an expedient by suggesting, off the reel, the propriety of the cabman's shelter, as it was called, hardly a stonesthrow away . . .

But there is a significant difference of tone. Joyce uses this tired language in 'Eumaeus' precisely because both Bloom and Stephen are tired after the events of the brothel district. The lights of fantasy flashed so vividly in 'Circe' that only a subdued light, proper for convalescence, may now be admitted. Hence the fagged tagmemes, the staleness of response to ideas and impressions. The chapter is very long and relentlessly cheerful (like a cub-reporter determined to get on); there is tiredness but not sleepiness. The nerves babble away and cannot stop, as if both Bloom and Stephen have been deprived of the muscular energy needed to staunch the flow with a single determined gesture. There is an ancient mariner in this section, a returned

Ulysses called Murphy, and he is the small god of a prose-style that holds us, as well as the bigger Ulysses, with an eye more lacklustre than glittering.

There is nothing weary about the style of 'Nausicaa'. The language is apt for a plebeian virgin, brought up on religion and niceness, who is eager to engage life:

Gerty MacDowell who was seated near her companions, lost in thought, gazing far away into the distance, was in very truth as fair a specimen of winsome Irish girlhood as one could wish to see. She was pronounced beautiful by all who knew her though, as folks often said, she was more a Giltrap than a MacDowell. Her figure was slight and graceful, inclining even to fragility but those iron jelloids she had been taking of late had done her a world of good much better than the Widow Welch's female pills and she was much better of those discharges she used to get and that tired feeling.

It will be observed that the style is made to admit a content unusual in novelettes or even in the more 'intimate' columns of magazines of the period (which would say: 'G.McD. – Send s.a.e. and I will write you personally on this problem'). The idiom has entered Gerty's very soul and is the medium of all her musings: we stand midway between an interior monologue and a *genre* narrative:

It was Gerty who turned off the gas at the main every night and it was Gerty who tacked up on the wall of that place where she never forgot every fortnight the chlorate of lime Mr Tunney the grocer's christmas almanac the picture of halcyon days where a young gentleman in the costume they used to wear then with a threecornered hat he was offering a bunch of flowers to his ladylove with oldtime chivalry through her lattice window.... She often looked at them dreamily when there for a certain purpose and felt her own arms that were white and soft just like hers ...

Even those euphemisms would be too much for Miss Cummins's *The Lamplighter* or *Mabel Vaughan*, works which Gerty has read. But sometimes the ladylikeness breaks down:

Gerty wished to goodness they would take their squalling baby home out of that and not get on her nerves no hour to be out and the little brats of twins.
Little monkeys common as ditchwater. Someone ought to take them and give them a good hiding for themselves to keep them in their places, the both of them.

When Gerty exhibits herself to Bloom, innocently enough by today's standards, the style is stretched to the limit. We come close to Molly's monologue, though it is always evident that this is a girl of seventeen, not a woman in her thirties:

... and she let him and she saw that he saw and then it went so high it went out of sight a moment and she was trembling in every limb for being bent so far back he had a full view high up above her knee no-one ever not even on the swing or wading and she wasn't ashamed and he wasn't either to look in that immodest way like that because he couldn't resist the sight of the wondrous revealment half offered like those skirtdancers behaving so immodest before gentlemen looking and he kept on looking, looking.

The 'it went so high' refers to the rocket being fired at the Mirus Bazaar which the viceroy opened. This firework display is highly convenient. It justifies Gerty's leaning back 'more and more to look up after it' and it provides a symbol for Bloom's consequent orgasm:

And then a rocket sprang and bang shot blind and O! then the Roman candle burst and it was like a sigh of O! and everyone cried O! O! in raptures and it gushed out of it a stream of rain gold hair threads and they shed and ah! they were all greeny dewy stars falling with golden, O so lovely! O so soft, sweet, soft!

This kind of impressionism is, of course, far ahead of the resources of Edwardian woman's journalism, but both meet in a common area of gushiness. Joyce has no difficulty, after Bloom's spasm, in resuming the main style:

Then all melted away dewily in the grey air: all was silent. Ah! She glanced at him as she bent forward quickly, a pathetic little glance of piteous protest, of shy reproach under which he coloured like a girl. He was leaning back against the rock behind. Leopold Bloom (for it is he) stands silent, with bowed head before those young guileless eyes. What a brute he had been! At it again? A fair unsullied soul had called to him and, wretch that he was, how had he answered? An utter cad he had been.

The cognate style of 'Eumaeus' maintains a certain distance from its protagonists. In its crass innocent way it also ensures that a certain distance is kept between these two, who have, at last, made contact: the event would seem to call for all the resources of Joycean prose-poetry at its richest, but the irony of the dénouement lies in the discovery that they have really so little in common. The prose, then, matches the situation at both the higher and lower levels. Occasionally, though, it seems ready to break down to admit the entry of an inarticulable complexity. Bloom has been telling Stephen about his encounter with the Cyclops.

He turned a long you are wrong gaze on Stephen of timorous dark pride at the soft impeachment, with a glance also of entreaty for he seemed to glean in a kind of way that it wasn't all exactly . . .

And, towards the end of the episode, Joyce modulates into something like his own narrative style (perhaps under the influence of a subject-matter the journalese is incompetent to deal with):

The horse was just then . . . and later on, at a propitious opportunity he purposed (Bloom did), without anyway prying into his private affairs on the *fools step in where angels* principle advising him to sever his connection with a certain budding practitioner, who, he noticed, was prone to disparage, and even, to a slight extent, with some hilarious pretext, when not present, deprecate him, or whatever you like to call it, which, in Bloom's humble opinion, threw a nasty sidelight on that side of a person's character – no pun intended.

The horse, having reached the end of his tether, so to speak, halted, and, rearing high a proud feathering tail, added his quota by letting fall on the floor, which the brush would soon brush up and polish, three smoking globes of turds. Slowly, three times, one after another, from a full crupper, he mired. And humanely the driver waited till he (or she) had ended, patient in his scythed car.

One may ask oneself how it is possible to read the long eventless chapter without becoming as weary as the convalescent Stephen. The answer is that the new, and mainly uncharacteristic, aspect of Bloom which the style itself imposes is extremely amusing; the skill with which Joyce avoids deviating into brightness has to be watched with the care accorded to a display of juggling; and the idiolect of the returned sailor Murphy is appallingly fascinating. Despite his name and home – Carrigaloe, Queenstown Harbour – he seems to have no Irish on him:

– Why, the sailor answered, upon reflection upon it, I've circumnavigated a bit since I first joined on. I was in the Red Sea. I was in China and North America and South America. I seen icebergs plenty, growlers. I was in Stockholm and the Black Sea, the Dardanelles, under Captain Dalton the best bloody man that ever scuttled a ship. I seen Russia.

Gospodi pomilooy. That's how the Russians prays. . . . I seen queer things too, ups and downs. I seen a crocodile bite the fluke of an anchor same as I chew that quid . . . And I seen maneaters in Peru that eats corpses and the livers of horses . . . Chews coca all day long, the communicative tarpaulin added. Stomachs like breadgraters. Cuts off their diddies when they can't bear no more children. See them there stark ballocknaked eating a dead horse's liver raw.

This first episode of the *Nostos* has, as its Homeric counterpart, the meeting between Odysseus and Telemachus in the hut of the swineherd Eumaeus. The hero was back in Ithaca, but in disguise, and such motifs as mistaken identity, mystery of name and provenance, lies, left-handedness (the left hand being the deceitful hand), impostors and pretenders – all of which fill the talk in the cabman's shelter – are appropriate to Joyce's symbolic intention. There is, beneath the cliché-bristling babble, a very intricate and wide-awake network of imaginative signals. As the nerves are the body's contribution to the presiding symbology, so the science figured here is navigation. This chapter is like a ship travelling through the night: it seems asleep but it knows precisely where it is going.

After the brief rest in the cabman's shelter, Bloom must re-possess Ithaca – No. 7 Eccles Street – and take Telemachus with him. They will drink cocoa, talk, look for the points of affinity which seem to have escaped them so far. In 'Eumaeus' Joyce seems to have reached the limit of humiliation of English prose. What is there left for him to do now? The mood is quiet and nocturnal, and soon we must all bed down with Penelope: there is no occasion for imaginative flights which will startle us into too much wakefulness. Joyce's solution is one of impersonalisation; the prose must be, if not quite dead, inhuman – the language of science. The particular science he chooses is statistics, which will enable some disembodied questioner to enquire into the relationship between Bloom and Stephen and receive the most comprehensive answers while learning nothing essential – that is to say, human. We are down now to the skeleton of the body, the enduring bone. But *enduring* is a relevant term here. The process of stripping Bloom and Stephen of flesh and blood miraculously elevates them to the status of stellar bodies: they endure as a father-son constellation in the heavens. Here is the eternising Gradgrind at work:

Of what did the duumvirate deliberate during their itinerary?

Music, literature, Ireland, Dublin, Paris, friendship, prostitution, diet, the influence of gaslight or the light of arc and glowlamps on the growth of adjoining paraheliotropic trees, exposed corporation emergency dustbuckets, the Roman catholic church, ecclesiastical celibacy, the Irish nation, jesuit education, careers, the study of medicine, the past day, the maleficent influence of the pre-sabbath, Stephen's collapse.

Among the facts that the inhuman catechist wants to know are, naturally enough, the 'common factors so similarity between their respective like and unlike reactions to experience'. The answer is:

Both were sensitive to artistic impressions musical in preference to plastic or pictorial. Both preferred a continental to an insular manner of life, a cisatlantic to a transatlantic place of residence. Both indurated by early domestic training and an inherited tenacity of heterodox resistance professed their disbelief in many orthodox religious, national, social and ethical doctrines. Both admitted the alternately stimulating and obtunding influence of heterosexual magnetism.

The grim style sometimes breaks down, approaching poetry against its will in the odd epithet:

Having set the halffilled kettle on the now burning coals, why did he return to the stillflowing tap?

To wash his soiled hands with a partially consumed tablet of Barrington's lemonflavoured soap, to which paper still adhered (bought thirteen hours previously for fourpence and still unpaid for), in fresh cold neverchanging everchanging water . . .

Or it trembles on the edge of an irrelevant elegance:

What in water did Bloom, waterlover, drawer of water, watercarrier returning to the range, admire?

Bloom relinquishes 'his symposiarchal right to the moustache cup of imitation Crown Derby presented to him by his only daughter, Millicent (Milly)' and serves himself cocoa in a cup identical with that he gives Stephen. The question asked is:

Was the guest conscious of and did he acknowledge these marks of hospitality?

And the answer is pure Joyce:

His attention was directed to them by his host jocosely and he accepted them seriously as they drank in jocoserious silence Epps's massproduct, the creature cocoa.*

When Stephen, escorted by Bloom goes through the garden preparatory to leaving, there is a flowering into poetry which has inspired at least one cantata and an operatic duet:

What spectacle confronted them when they, first the host, then the guest, emerged silently, doubly dark, from obscurity by a passage from the rere of the house into the penumbra of the garden?
The heaventree of stars hung with humid nightblue fruit.

But, for several pages thereafter, we are given indigestible astronomical facts which only our knowledge of Stephen's and Bloom's impending apotheosis can make us spoon down.

When Stephen has left, the catechist turns his or its searchlight on the house itself (after all, this is Ithaca), Bloom's possessions, Bloom's ambitions, even Bloom's toenails, and then follows Bloom into the bedroom, where a moment of tenderness is admitted:

He kissed the plump mellow yellow smellow melons of her rump, on each plump melonous hemisphere, in their mellow yellow furrow, with obscure prolonged provocative melonsmellonous osculation.

But, when Bloom is in bed, the answerer grows sleepy:

Womb? Weary?
    He rests. He has travelled.
    With?
Sinbad the Sailor and Tinbad the Tailor and Jinbad the Jailer and Whinbad the Whaler and Ninbad the Nailer and Finbad the Failer and Binbad the Bailer and Pinbad the Pailer and Minbad the Mailer and Hinbad the Hailer and Rinbad the Railer and Dinbad the Kailer and Vinbad the Quailer and Linbad the Yailer and Xinbad the Phthailer.
    When?
Going to a dark bed there was a square round Sinbad the Sailor roc's auk's egg in the night of the bed of all the auks of the rocs of Darkinbad the Brightdayler.
    Where?

Some editions of *Ulysses* give an enlarged black dot as the answer to this last question, and this may be interpreted, in reading

* I do not think we have to take too seriously Professor Tindall's suggestion that 'mass' here has three meanings, one of them religious.

aloud, as a grunt or a snore. Knowing that nothing in Joyce is
ever arbitrary or casual, it is in order to speculate on the sub-
merged meaning in the 'Sinbad the Sailor' nonsense.* Even on
the surface it is not quite nonsense, since Bloom is established as
an adventurous voyager whose origins lie in the East, not the
West. The rhymes that follow list genuine trades or personal
characteristics and may be taken as a reasonable summing-up of
the many kinds of men a voyager will encounter (one is not sure
about 'Yailer' and 'Phthailer', though the latter may be a hailer
with phthisis). The final articulate or near-articulate answer
alludes to a genuine adventure of Sinbad's and seems to make
Bloom put a square – symbol of control or order – about an
emblem of life which may or may not be malevolent (the auk,
anyway, is a real bird of the North). Finally, out of the bad dark
the bright day reemerges, and the myths and the realities have
to be engaged once more. Perhaps all this is going too far.

* Professor Robert Martin Adams believes this to be a reminiscence from a
Christmas pantomime Joyce saw when he was a child.

CHAPTER 8

The Language of Gestation

🐍🐍🐍🐍🐍

THE whole of *Ulysses* celebrates the art of literature, and its presidency over the 'Scylla and Charybdis' chapter is supererogatory. This chapter establishes a very tenuous parallelism between fictional content and Homeric counterpart. We have, in Stephen's disquisition on the relationship of Shakespeare's life and work, the bard's steering between the rock of home and the whirlpool of London, and with his wife's infidelity, the collapse of all solidity except that of his art:

Christfox in leather trews, hiding, a runaway in blighted treeforks from hue and cry. Knowing no vixen, walking lonely in the chase. Women he won to him, tender people, a whore of Babylon, ladies of justices, bully tapsters' wives. Fox and geese. And in New Place, a slack dishonoured body that once was comely, once as sweet, as fresh as cinnamon, now her leaves falling, all bare, frighted of the narrow grave and unforgiven.

We have also the wishy-washy, mystical, theosophical insubstantiality of Irish art, with George Russell (AE) burbling about the universals of Plato, against which whirlpool Stephen sets the solidity of his own art (the above is a sample) and the hard Scyllan rock of Aristotelian logic. As for the formal scope of literature – which one would expect to be demonstrated at one level or another – we have little except specimens of blank verse which, on Stephen's drinkfilled foodempty stomach, quickly leave the five-foot rock and swirl:

> And therefore he left out her name
> From the first draft but he did not leave out
> The presents for his granddaughter, for his daughters,
> For his sister, for his old cronies in Stratford
> And in London. And therefore when he was urged,

As I believe, to name her
He left her his
Secondbest
Bed.

Punkt

Leftherhis
Secondbest
Bestabed
Secabest
Leftabed.
Woa!

The special celebration of English literature appears where we least expect it – in the scene where Bloom visits the Holles Street lying-in hospital to enquire about the welfare of his wife's friend Mrs Purefoy, who is waiting, with pain and difficulty, for an addition to an already large family. Fecundity is the theme, and the Homeric parallel is to be found in the blasphemy of the followers of Odysseus, who, in their hunger, slew and ate the oxen of the sungod Phoebus. The oxen were divinely fertile and, as emblems of fertility, they bellow through the chapter. Their slaughter is effected symbolically by some medical students Bloom meets in the hospital, who, in their cups, speak loudly about the virtue of separating the act of sex from the divine true end of procreation. As Odysseus's men were struck down for their crime by the thunderbolt of Zeus, so the students are temporarily daunted by the thunder of Dublin's heaven. There is a heavy shower of rain in this episode, an assertion of fecundity. There is also the presence of Bloom, a father looking for a son. And there is the son himself, drunken Stephen, who blasphemes, but not against the oxen. He is on the side of fertility – art itself being a manifestation of creative lust – and he has even, many hundreds of pages previously, dubbed himself 'bullockbefriending bard'. Mr Deasy, owner of the school where Stephen has been teaching, asked him to place with his 'literary friends' a letter proposing new methods of dealing with foot and mouth disease. The bull – as alpha or aleph – is the first letter of the alphabet, without which literature would be impossible: here is a thin connection between a maternity hospital and a library. But Joyce's imagination is equal to a stronger ligature than that.

The art which rules the chapter is medicine, chiefly in its obstetrical aspect, and the style in which it is written was termed by Joyce *embryological*. He wishes to represent the growth of the foetus in the womb, from conception to the moment of birth, and he decides to do this through a sort of fantastic history of English prose. His first task, though, is to make ritual homage to the oxen of fertility, the sungod to whom they belong, and the miracle of birth over which they preside. He begins with triple invocations in the manner of the *Fratres Arvales*:

Deshil Holles Eamus. Deshil Holles Eamus. Deshil Holles Eamus.

Send us, bright one, light one, Horhorn, quickening and womb-fruit. Send us, bright one, light one, Horhorn, quickening and womb-fruit. Send us, bright one, light one, Horhorn, quickening and womb-fruit.

Hoopsa, boyaboy, hoopsa! Hoopsa, boyaboy, hoopsa! Hoopsa, boyaboy, hoopsa!

First, it is suggested that we go to Holles Street off Denzille, or Deshil, Lane. Then the sun is addressed prayerfully. The 'Horhorn' comes straight from Blazes Boylan's jingling music, turning him into an ironic god of fecundity (but he blazes and boils), and it stands both for an erection and the double cornution of the bulls. Finally, a boy is born: he is lifted to the air and there are cries of glee.

We move at once to three ghastly paragraphs written in the following style:

Universally that person's acumen is esteemed very little perceptive concerning whatsoever matters are being held as most profitably by mortals with sapience endowed to be studied who is ignorant of that which the most in doctrine erudite and certainly by reason of that in them high mind's ornament deserving of veneration constantly maintain when by general consent they affirm that other circumstances being equal by no exterior splendour is the prosperity of a nation more efficaciously asserted than by the measure of how far forward may have progressed the tribute of its solicitude for that proliferent continuance which of evils the original if it be absent when fortunately present constitutes the certain sign of omnipollent nature's incorrupted benefaction.

The structure and the vocabulary alike are Latinate, and the whole reads like a grotesque travesty of a Cicero already grotesquely travestying himself. Joyce said that his opening paragraphs were intended to be in the manner of Sallust, but Sallust was neat and elegant, and this is not (perhaps Joyce was punning on the saltness of lust); nor is it intended to be. We have here, unformed, unfertilised, the feminine element of the English language awaiting the ministrations of bullish Anglo-Saxon. Its coming is delayed while Irish hospitals are praised – 'O thing of prudent nation,' etc – and the coming seems premature:

Before born babe bliss had. Within womb won he worship. Whatever in that one case done commodiously done was . . . not omitting aspect of all very distracting spectacles in various latitudes by our terrestrial orb offered . . .

But with the appearance of Bloom as phallus (he whips off his hat on entering) the Germanic settles in without a Latinism to be seen:

Some man that wayfaring was stood by housedoor at night's oncoming. Of Israel's folk was that man that on earth wandering far had fared. Stark ruth of man his errand that him lone led till that house.

'Of that house,' we learn, 'A. Horne is lord' – an historically verifiable fact and very convenient for Joyce's symbolism. Bloom is granted admittance, the door of the interns' common room opens, and young Dr Dixon, who had once attended Bloom when stung by a bee, invites him in for a drink. We move at once into the English of Malory:

And in the castle was set a board that was of the birchwood of Finlandy and it was upheld by four dwarfmen of that country but they durst not move more for enchantment . . . And full fair cheer and rich was on the board that no wight could devise a fuller ne richer. And there was a vat of silver that was moved by craft to open in the which lay strange fishes withouten heads though misbelieving men nie that this be possible thing without they see it natheless they are so. And these fishes lie in an oily water brought there from Portugal land because of the fatness that therein is like to the juices of the olive press.

The can of sardines thus periphrastically described has a significance in terms of the embryological history figured in the literary one: it is at this stage of development (the first or Malory month) that the foetus is itself a fish, asleep in a vat of amniotic fluid. The progress of the foetus is not uniform, as a sudden inconsistency in the prose attests:

And sir Leopold that was the goodliest guest that ever sat in scholars' hall and that was the meekest man and the kindest that ever laid husbandly hand under hen and that was the very truest knight of the world one that ever did minion service to lady gentle pledged him courtly in the cup. Woman's woe with wonder pondering.

We plunge back without warning to an earlier stage of linguistic development, as parts of the embryo undergo structural retrogression. But Joyce has to point this prosodically, introducing an imitation of an Anglo-Saxon line of verse: to go the whole linguistic hog would be too much in a work of fictional entertainment. Note the reference to Sir Leopold's 'husbandly hand under hen', which takes the reader back to the narrator's jibe in the 'Cyclops' chapter.

In a kind of early Tudor English Stephen – 'that had mien of a frere that was at head of the board' – defines the sin against the Holy Ghost, which seems to be contraception:

Murmur, sirs, is eke oft among lay folk. Both babe and parent now glorify their Maker, the one in limbo gloom, the other in purge fire. But, gramercy, what of those Godpossibled souls that we nightly impossibilise, which is the sin against the Holy Ghost, Very God, Lord and Giver of Life? For sirs, he said, our lust is brief. We are means to those small creatures within us and nature has other ends than we.

He for one does not appear to be blaspheming against the oxen. He informs the company that the soul is infused into the embryo in the second month and, by a very irregular and macaronic route, leads us into Elizabethan English:

He gave them then a much admirable hymen minim by those delicate poets Master John Fletcher and Master Francis Beaumont that is in their *Maid's Tragedy* that was writ for a like twining of lovers: *To bed, to bed*, was the burden of it to be played with accompanable concent upon the virginals.

Nietzsche is invoked some centuries too early, and the condom is mentioned along with embryonic caudation, beef-flavoured:

Greater love than this, he said, no man hath that a man lay down his wife for his friend. Go thou and do likewise. Thus, or words to that effect, said Zarathustra, sometime regius professor of French letters to the university of Oxtail nor breathed there ever that man to whom mankind was more beholden.

We are now into the seventeenth century. Israel, harking back to a piece of oratory declaimed in 'AEolus', becomes Ireland and is vilified in the language of the King James version:

Remember, Erin, thy generations and thy days of old, how thou settedst little by me and by my word and broughtest in a stranger to my gates to commit fornication in my sight and to wax fat and kick like Jeshurum. Therefore hast thou sinned against the light and hast made me, thy lord, to be the slave of servants ... Why hast thou done this abomination before me that thou didst spurn me for a merchant of jalaps and didst deny me to the Roman and the Indian of dark speech with whom thy daughters did lie luxuriously?

The merchant of jalaps is the father of Haines, Stephen's *bête noire* of the tower. ('His old fellow made his tin,' according to Mulligan, 'by selling jalap to Zulus or some bloody swindle or other.') Sir Thomas Browne comes immediately after – indeed, in the same paragraph –

Assuefaction minorates atrocities (as Tully saith of his darling Stoics) and Hamlet his father showeth the prince no blister of combustion. The adiaphane in the noon of life is an Egypt's plague which in the nights of prenativity and postmortemity is their most proper *ubi* and *quomodo*.

– and then the sudden thunder rushes us back to atavistic fear and ancient language:

A black crack of noise in the street here, alack, bawled, back. Loud on left Thor thundered: in anger awful the hammerhurler.

Bloom, the calm rationalist, assures Stephen – who has been loud in his cups, though not against fertility (but is not the Christian God he mocks – 'old Nobodaddy' – a God of fertility?) – that the 'hubbub noise' is 'all of the order of a natural phenomenon', but Stephen is not comforted. This, of course, is Joyce himself, the lifelong thunderfearer. Very appositely, Bunyan's *Pilgrim's Progress* provides a Godfearing style for everybody, rechristening Stephen as Young Boasthard and Bloom as Cautious Calmer. The leching sinners of the assembly have provided themselves with contraceptives, mocking at 'the god Bringforth':

... Preservative had given them a stout shield of oxengut ... that they might take no hurt neither from Offspring that was that wicked devil by virtue of this same shield which was named Killchild.

And then a Restoration diary entry, neither Pepys nor Evelyn, gives us a weather report and, in cinematic style, cuts in effect to NEXT NIGHT and the approach of Mulligan:

Over against the Rt. Hon. Mr Justice Fitzgibbon's door (that is to sit with Mr Healy the lawyer upon the college lands) Mal. Mulligan a gentleman's gentleman that had but come from Mr Moore's the writer's (that was a papish but is now, folk say, a good Williamite) chanced against Alec. Bannon in a cut bob (which are now in with dance cloaks of Kendal green) that was new got to town from Mullingar with the stage where his coz and Mal M's brother will stay a month yet till Saint Swithin and asks what the earth he does there, he bound home and he to Andrew Horne's being stayed for to crush a cup of wine, so he said, but would tell him of a skittish heifer, big of her age and beef to the heel and all this while poured with rain and so both together on to Horne's.

If, by this time, we are disposed to admire the mimicry but to deplore the mimic's ceasing to be a novelist, we ought to pay close attention to such little revelations as are contained in the pastiches. Here, for instance, is a follow-up from the first chapter, where Mulligan said that his brother was down in Westmeath with the Bannons. He was told, by an anonymous swimmer, that Bannon had 'found a sweet young thing down there. Photo girl he calls her.' The photo girl is Bloom's own daughter Milly, who writes her father a letter saying:

We did great biz yesterday. Fair day and all the beef to the heels were in ... There is a young student comes here some evenings named Bannon his cousins or something are big swells he sings Boylan's (I was on the pop of writing Blazes Boylan's) song about those seaside girls ...

Fulfilling her father's frustrated scientific bent, Milly works in a photographer's shop. She is getting around and meeting people and has, however remotely, effected a connection between Bloom and Stephen through Bannon and Mulligan. She also helps to associate Bloom's Antinous (Boylan) with Stephen's (Mulligan) through her mention of the song Bannon sings. She anticipates the oxen theme with her 'beef to the heels', though this cruelly bounces back in the seventeenth-century report of her: 'a skittish heifer, big of her age and beef to the heel'. I for one refuse to believe she is thick-ankled: there is too much Central European and Mediterranean blood there. Anyway, here is Bannon in person, tightening a knot in the fabric.

Joyce, who has started somewhat prematurely to write like Swift, is evidently happier with the prose-styles of the Enlightenment than with earlier God-troped ones. A long discussion of the foot and mouth disease (Lenehan comes 'to the feet of the table to say how the letter was in that night's gazette' – Mr Deasy's letter) leads to a tale of an Irish – taurine – bull which is in a very racy idiom that combines Urquhart's Rabelais (thrusting us back to the pre-1660 era, since Urquhart is said to have died of joy on Charles II's accession) and Swift's *Tale of a Tub*. But this is a mere prelude to the entrance of Mulligan, accompanied by Bannon, who – in a generalised eighteenth-century fictional style that owes more to Smollett than to Fielding – puts forward the project of 'a national fertilising farm to be named *Omphalos*' and hands round cards with the legend *Mr Malachi Mulligan, Fertiliser and Incubator, Lambay Island*. That earlier Hellenic proposal has undergone a certain change. It is curious, too, to see how Mulligan, who belongs to the 'brood of mockers', has become the very voice of increase: in the Laurence Sterne pastiche which over-coyly celebrates contraception, he is named Le Fécondateur:

But beshrew me, he cried, clapping hand to his forehead, tomorrow will be a new day and, thousand thunders, I know of a *marchand de capotes*, Monsieur Poyntz, from whom I can have for a *livre* as snug a cloak of the French fashion as ever kept a lady from wetting. Tut, Tut! cries Le Fécondateur, tripping in, my friend Monsieur Moore, that most accomplished traveller (I have just cracked a half bottle *avec lui* in a circle of the best wits of the town), is my authority that in Cape Horn, *ventre biche*, they have a rain that will wet through any, even the stoutest cloak . . . Pooh! A *livre*! cries Monsieur Lynch. The clumsy things are dear at a sou. One umbrella, were it no bigger than a fairy mushroom, is worth ten such stopgaps . . .

We move through the style of the *Letters of Junius* (an unexpected and very bitter attack on Bloom's sexual *mores*) to a Gibbonian announcement of the birth of Mrs Purefoy's child. But the joy that should suffuse the company is swallowed in a fiery 'display of that discursiveness which seemed the only bond of union among tempers so divergent':

Every phase of the situation was successively eviscerated: the prenatal repugnance of uterine brothers, the Caesarean section, posthumity

with respect to the father and, that rarer form, with respect to the
mother, the fratricidal case known as the Childs murder and rendered
memorable by the impassioned plea of Mr Advocate Bushe which
secured the acquittal of the wrongfully accused, the rights of primo-
geniture and king's bounty touching twins and triplets, miscarriages
and infanticides, simulated and dissimulated, acardiac *foetus in foetu*,
aprospoia due to a congestion . . .

The amount of medical knowledge disclosed here – clinical and
forensic – is, of course, justified by the presiding science,* but
Joyce cunningly introduces the punning theme of the Childs
murder – mentioned earlier in the funeral and 'AEolus' chapters,
especially with regard to the skill of Seymour Bushe – so as to
have a horrifying content ready for his Gothick pastiche, which
comes next. Haines appears with one line essential to the narrative;
he tells Mulligan to meet him at Westland row station at ten past
eleven. For the rest, he is straight out of *The Castle of Otranto*.

Surprise, horror, loathing, were depicted on all faces while he eyed
them with a ghastly grin. I anticipated some such reception, he began
with an eldritch laugh, for which, it seems, history is to blame. Yes,
it is true. I am the murderer of Samuel Childs. And how I am punished!
The inferno has no terrors for me . . . Ah! Destruction! The black
panther! . . . The sage repeated *Lex talionis*. The sentimentalist is he
who would enjoy without incurring the immense debtorship for a
thing done. Malachias, overcome by emotion, ceased. The mystery
was unveiled. Haines was the third brother. His real name was Childs.
The black panther was himself the ghost of his own father . . .

This paragraph is crammed with references to the earlier part of
the book. In 'AEolus', Bushe's speech on the *lex talionis* is
quoted; Stephen, instead of meeting Haines and Mulligan at the
Ship, armed with his pint-buying wages, sent a telegram instead:
'The sentimentalist is he, etc.'; the black panther is the one that
has haunted Haines's dreams: 'the ghost of his own father' is
taken from Mulligan's mockery of Stephen's theory about
Hamlet. Musicalisation is as much at work here as in the chapter
to come – 'Circe'. After a rather moving paragraph in the style
of Charles Lamb, which laments Bloom's sonlessness – 'No son
of thy loins is by thee. There is none now to be for Leopold, what

---

* And its essentially nineteenth-century character is justified by the anticipa-
  tory jumps of the embryo.

Leopold was for Rudolph', Rudolph being Bloom's father – Joyce reaches the limit of his development of odd scraps and orts in an imitation of Thomas de Quincey:

Onward to the dead sea they tramp to drink, unslaked and with horrible gulpings, the salt somnolent inexhaustible flood. And the equine portent grows again, magnified in the deserted heavens, nay to heaven's own magnitude, till it looms, vast, over the house of Virgo. And lo, wonder of metempsychosis, it is she, the everlasting bride, harbinger of the daystar, the bride, ever virgin. It is she, Martha, thou lost one, Millicent, the young, the dear, the radiant. How serene does she now arise, a queen among the Pleiades, in the penultimate antelucan hours, shod in sandals of bright gold, coifed with a veil of what do you call it gossamer! It floats, it flows about her starborn flesh and loose it streams emerald, sapphire, mauve and heliotrope, sustained on currents of cold interstellar wind, winding, coiling, simply swirling writhing in the skies a mysterious writing till after a myriad metamorphoses of symbol, it blazes, Alpha, a ruby and triangled sign upon the forehead of Taurus.

This is an evocation of the ancestral East Bloom thought briefly about in the morning, reading his 'Agendath Netaim' advertisement. The dead sea is all his. The 'equine portent' refers to the Gold Cup winner Throwaway; the virginal references mix Milly Bloom, Martha Clifford and Gerty MacDowell. The word 'metempsychosis', dissected into 'met him pike hoses' by Molly, we met first in the 'Calypso' chapter. 'Martha, thou lost one' refers to Mr Dedalus's singing in 'Sirens' of '*M'appari*' from *Martha* ,with its line 'Come, thou lost one, come, thou dear one'. The morning light is to Mr Bloom a girl in gold sandals; soon he works out costumes for all phases of the day, thinking of Ponchielli's 'Dance of the Hours'. 'Simply swirling' comes from Boylan's song, remembered by Bloom, referred to in Milly's letter, about the seaside girls. Alpha is confused with delta, but very reasonably, since the island of the sun-oxen, Sicily, is triangular. Why 'ruby'? Because there are bottles of Bass on the table, and these have on their labels the red triangle trade mark. This is the way Joyce so often works, especially in *Finnegans Wake*. Form is what he loves, and it seems a pity that – unlike music – prose form cannot subsist without content. But Joyce's content is as limited, in terms of the separable and summarisable, as ingenuity can make it. He is, as we know, McLuhan's delight.

Joyce's nineteenth century runs through science as well as sentiment, and settles to a glorification of Purefoy the father, first in the manner of Dickens:

He is older now (you and I may whisper it) and a trifle stooped in the shoulders yet in the whirligig of years a grave dignity has come to the conscientious second accountant of the Ulster bank, College Green branch. O Doady, loved one of old, faithful lifemate now, it may never be again, that faroff time of the roses! With the old shake of her pretty head she recalls those days. God, how beautiful now across the mist of years! But their children are grouped in her imagination about the bedside, hers and his, Charley, Mary Alice, Frederick Albert (if he had lived), Mamy, Budgy (Victoria Frances), Tom, Violet Constance Louisa, darling little Bobsy (called after our famous hero of the South African war, lord Bobs of Waterford and Candahar) and now this last pledge of their union, a Purefoy if ever there was one, with the true Purefoy nose.

Finally in the style of Carlyle:

Twenty years of it, regret them not. With thee it was not as with many that will and would and wait and never do. Thou sawest thy America, thy lifetask, and didst charge to cover like the transpontine bison. How saith Zarathustra? *Deine Kuh Trübsal melkest Du. Nun Trinkst Du die süsse Milch des Euters.* See! It displodes for thee in abundance. Drink, man, an udderful! Mother's milk, Purefoy, the milk of human kin, milk too of those burgeoning stars overhead, rutilant in thin rain-vapour, punch milk, such as those rioters will quaff in the guzzlingden, milk of madness, the honeymilk of Canaan's land. Thy cow's dug was tough, what? Ay, but her milk is hot and sweet and fattening. No dollop this but thick rich bonnyclaber. To her, old patriarch! Pap! *Per deam Partulam et Pertundam nunc est bibendum!*

Purefoy has himself become an ox. Joyce, to match the Purefoy baby's thrusting itself into the fresh air of the dirty world, now sends the entire company off to Burke's pub for a last drink before closing-time. A history of literature provided a parallel for the gestatory process, but now gestation is at an end and literature must end also. The world that the baby greets is expressed in language which, though creative enough, is most unliterary. The reader has the problem of discovering what is happening among the characters by scrambling through thickets of slang, pidgin, dialect and various kinds of cant term. It is still apparently raining: 'Any brollies or gumboots in the fambly?' Stephen is, as later in 'Circe', taken for a clergyman: 'Jay, look at the drunken minister coming out of the maternity hospital.' Bloom is evidently invited along: 'Yous join uz, dear sir? No hentrusion in life. Lou heap good man. Allee samee this bunch.' And so on their way: 'Fire away number one on the gun. Burke's! Thence they advanced five parasangs.'

The mock-military tone is maintained for a time:

Tention. Proceed to nearest canteen and there annex liquor stores. March! Tramp, tramp, tramp the boys are (attitudes!) parching. Beer, beef, business, bibles, bulldogs, battleships, buggery and bishops. Whether on the scaffold high. Beerbeef trample the bibles. When for Irelandear. Trample the trampellers. Thunderation! Keep the durned millingtary step. We fall. Bishops' boosebox. Halt! Heave to. Rugger. Scrum in. No touch kicking. Wow, my tootsies! You hurt? Most amazingly sorry!

In the pub we hear the voice of Mulligan clearly enough:

Ours the white death and the ruddy birth ... Mummer's wire. Cribbed out of Meredith. Jesified orchidised polycimical jesuit! Aunty mine's writing Pa Kinch. Baddybad Stephen lead astray goody-good Malachi.

The first reference is to Mulligan's conversation with Haines in the D.B.C. teashop: Stephen, having being scared out of his wits by visions of hell, can never be a poet, says Mulligan: the Swinburnian note of 'the white death and the ruddy birth' is beyond him. Then Stephen ('Kinch, the loveliest mummer of them all') is alleged to have cribbed his telegram about the sentimentalist from George Meredith. Finally we have the irony of crossed letters. Mr Dedalus has already expressed the intention of writing to Mulligan's aunt complaining about his corruption of Stephen; the aunt is going to write to 'Pa Kinch' in diametrically opposed terms.

Bloom, the cautious, will take only a ginger cordial. This leads to some mockery and interesting information about what the medicals at the Mater Misericordiae see in the upper windows of No. 7 Eccles Street (the hospital is very close to Bloom's house):

Digs up near the Mater. Buckled he is. Know his dona? Yup, sartin, I do. Full of a dure. See her in her dishybilly. Peels off a credit. Lovely lovekin. None of your lean kine, not much. Pull down the blind, love.

Got a prime pair of mincepies, no kid. And her take me to rests and her anker of rum. Must be seen to be believed. Your starving eyes and allbeplastered neck you stole my heart, O gluepot. Sir? Spud again the rheumatiz? All poppycock, you'll scuse me saying.

Joyce's rhyming-slang seems unauthentic. Cockneys would prefer *Bristol cities and bottle and glass* or *Bristols and aris*. The reference to the anti-rheumatic potato that Bloom carries in his back-pocket is timely, since he will need a counterpart to Ulysses's moly before venturing into Circe country. Bloom finally takes something stronger than ginger cordial – wine in Romany – and is identified by Bannon as the father or 'papli' (Milly's word) of the photo-girl:

Rome boose for the Bloom toff. I hear you say onions? Bloo? Cadges ads? Photo's papli, by all that's gorgeous!

The man in the mackintosh, noticed by Bloom at the funeral that morning, makes another mysterious appearance:

Golly, whatten tunket's yon guy in the mackintosh? Dusty Rhodes. Peep at his wearables. By mighty! What's he got? Jubilee mutton. Bovril, by James. Wants it real bad. D'ye ken bare socks? Seedy cuss in the Richmond? Rawthere! Thought he had a deposit of lead in his penis. Trumpery insanity. Bartle the Bread we calls him. That, sir, was once a prosperous cit. Man all tattered and torn that married a maiden all forlorn. Slung her hook, she did. Here see lost love. Walking Mackintosh of lonely canyon.

Someone is now calling Bloom by his first name, or a truncation of it:

Pardon? See him today at runefal? Chum o yourn passed in his checks? Ludamassy! Pore picaninnies! Thou'll no be telling me thot, Pold veg! Did ums blubble bigsplash crytears cos frien Padney was took off in black bag?

And then we learn that Stephen, who has been drinking absinthe – the 'greeneyed monster' as Bloom calls it later – is on his way, with Lynch, to Mabbot Street:

Lynch! Hey? Sign on long o me. Denzille lane this way. Change here for Bawdyhouse. We two, she said, will seek the kips where shady Mary is. Righto, any old time. *Laetabuntur in cubilibus suis.*

We do not learn that Bloom follows Stephen, paternally concerned as he is, until the following chapter, when everybody has arrived at 'the Mabbot street entrance of nighttown'. It is this lack of essential narrative information that is most likely to make the reader murmur. An intolerable deal of sack and not even a halfpennyworth of bread. And this is a crucial scene, the one in which Bloom, seeing Stephen drunk and among enemies, conceives a fatherly love potent enough to drive him to strange and dangerous places.

Joyce's technique can, as always, be justified. He needs an objective narrative style, or series of styles, and since he has already used or pre-empted for future use the colloquial and the journalistic, there is not really much else available except pastiche of past styles. In the 'Cyclops' chapter he used some of these effectively, especially the Scottian Wardour Street:

Our travellers reached the rustic hostlery and alighted from their palfreys.
– Ho, varlet! cried he, who by his mien seemed the leader of the party. Saucy knave! To us!
So saying he knocked loudly with his swordhilt upon the open lattice.
Mine host came forth at the summons girding him with his tabard.
– Give you good den, my masters, said he with an obsequious bow.
– Bestir thyself, sirrah! cried he who had knocked. Look to our steeds. And for ourselves give us of your best for ifaith we need it.

But, so that he shall not repeat himself, he must make the comedy of the 'Oxen of the Sun' episode derive not from the disparity between human pretension and human capability – expressed in sudden inflation and deflation as sudden – but from the inability of the language of the past to encompass the referents of the present. And the strain we feel, trying to follow the story of Bloom's non-consubstantial fatherhood through language never intended to express it, is cognate with the hopelessness, a very resigned and humorous hopelessness, that comes with 'Eumaeus' and the Ithacan catechism. No real father-son rapprochement is possible between Stephen and Bloom, but at least the 'Oxen' language is striving to establish one. Both characters are caught up in a process which curiously ennobles them – the wonder of the growth of the embryo expressed in the wonder of the growth of a national literature. It is essentially a man's literature, even bullish in its occasional aggressiveness, fulfilling one view of art as a kind of 'paternity lust'. If the chapter seems to go on too long, that is because Joyce, in these later episodes of the novel, insists on making the reading time the same, roughly, as the imagined time of enactment. No lacunae, no summaries.

The parallel between the growth of a foetus and the growth of a language does not really work, nor is it maintained consistently. The child is born about 1750 and the literary styles roll on until, at the latest, 1881. The cunningly planted references to oxen and to the various achieved stages of embryonic development are a Joycean self-indulgence and few readers notice them or, if noticing, care. But the whole chapter is curiously satisfying, chiefly because Joyce makes it appear that *Ulysses* not merely continues the line of literature in English but encloses it as well. And as a virtuoso display it dazzles, confirming a suspicion already pretty firmly held that Joyce can do anything with language.

CHAPTER 9

Onomastics

🕱🕱🕱🕱🕱🕱

IN the 'Cyclops' chapter, reporting journalistically a meeting on the revival of 'ancient Gaelic sports', Joyce ends with the following:

Amongst the clergy present were the very rev. William Delany, S.J., L.L.D.; the rt rev. Gerald Molloy, D.D.; the rev. P. J. Kavanagh, C.S. Sp.; the rev. T. Waters, C.C.; the rev. John M. Ivers, P.P.; the rev P. J. Cleary, O.S.F.; the rev. L. J. Hickey, O.P.; the very rev. Fr. Nicholas, O.S.F.C.; the very rev. B. Gorman, O.D.C.; the rev. T. Maher, S.J.; the very rev. James Murphy, S.J.; the rev. John Lavery, V.F.; the very rev. William Doherty, D.D.; the rev. Peter Fagan, O.M.; the rev. T. Brangan, O.S.A.; the rev. J. Flavin, C.C.; the rev. M. A. Hacket, C.C.; the rev. W. Hurley, C.C.; the rt rev. Mgr Mc-Manus, V.G.; the rev. B. R. Slattery, O.M.I.; the very rev. M. D. Scally, P.P.; the rev. F. T. Purcell, O.P.; the very rev. Timothy canon Gorman, P.P.; the rev. J. Flanagan, C.C. The laity included P. Fay, T. Quirke, etc., etc.

A lesser author, wishing to satirise the Irish worship of the clergy, would have provided this assembly with comic names, on the lines of Ben Jonson or Charles Dickens. But to Joyce the ordinary Irish name, especially if ennobled with an honorific before and letters after, condemns its owner to a despicable drabness. English names like Armstrong, Drinkwater, Godsave and Brewer exhibit an etymology and carry an image and a colour, but the names of Joyce's Dubliners are mere counters that, to all but the Gaelic scholar, show nothing of their origin in trade or topography or ancestral idiosyncrasy. Conor Cruise O'Brien reminds us that the period between the death of Parnell in 1891 and the Easter rising of 1916 was a drab interregnum. Yeats, after 1916, could memorialise names like MacDonagh and MacBride and Connolly and Pearse in heroic verse, but to Joyce, who recorded only that interregnum, Irish names had little of nobility about

them. Young Stephen Dedalus sees the name of the pandying
Prefect of Studies – Dolan – as appropriate to a washerwoman,
while his own is great and classical, something out of a Roman
senatorial rollcall (strange that no member of his family has yet
told him that it is the name of the fabulous artificer). It is surprising that Joyce should, when first planning his autobiographical novel, have thought of calling his hero Murphy; on the other
hand, names like Murphy and Molloy do well enough in the
writings of Samuel Beckett. It is the combination of naturalism
and symbolism in Joyce, sometimes blending with each other
uneasily, that makes his approach to proper names different
from that of any other writer.

The names of the characters in *Dubliners* match the poverty of
their lives. It is only in the final story, 'The Dead', that we meet a
personage who is a cut above the Lenehans and McCoys. This
is Gabriel Conroy the writer, closer to Joyce in trade, temperament and ambition than anyone we have met so far. When we
enter the strange world of the universal snow and learn, with
him, that his wife Gretta once loved a young consumptive 'in
the gasworks' and that his name was Michael Furey, then proper
names – for the first time in Joyce's writing – take on a symbolic
function. For Michael is the 'furious' angel, while Gabriel is the
mild one. But, we have only recently discovered, Joyce did not
choose Gabriel's name because of this connotation. He got the
idea of the snow from a short story by Bret Harte, and the title
of the story is 'Gabriel Conroy'. Joyce sometimes paid his
debts. Sometimes, too, he was lucky. Eccles Street, where Leopold Bloom had his residence before they pulled it down in
1965, begins like the Latin word *ecclesia*. In the first chapter of
Ulysses, Stephen rejects the Church along with his family, but a
visual pun leads him to a kind of substitute for both.

A Portrait, like *Dubliners*, is full of base Irish names. The base-
ness is that of the common earth (in which murphies grow), and
the hero must rise above it into the bright air. In the first draft
of the novel, his name was spelt 'Dædalus': the digraph sticks
up like a sore thumb. 'Dedalus' fits not too badly into the
naturalistic texture, especially as some other names tremble on
the verge of the symbolic. Simon Moonan is guilty of a mild
form of simony, and Stephen's own father – who has sold his
intelligence and his God-given artistic potentialities for drink – is

also Simon. The effeminate boy called Tusker Boyle (sometimes Lady Boyle, because he is always paring his nails) provides a sexual overtone for Stephen's broodings on ivory – first ('Tower of ivory') as an item in the Litany, later as a word to be considered in its own right as a poetic wonder. Stephen's name has evidently been well thought out. Stephen was the protomartyr; his namesake will become a martyr for art (not the first martyr, unfortunately, since Gustave Flaubert pre-empted that distinction for himself). The fabulous artificer Dædalus or Dedalus is invoked by Stephen as a father. This turns him into Icarus. Icarus is a winged being falling from heaven. So is Lucifer. Stephen, with Lucifer, has said '*Non serviam*'. He is not afraid, he says, of losing his soul in the service of bringing light through art. But he refuses to register the image of Icarus. He Freudianly gets Nashe's line wrong, remembering it as 'Darkness falls from the air'.

Ulysses, being full of Dubliners, is full of very ordinary names. The name of the hero is ordinary enough, by the standards of diasporal Jewry. 'Bloom', a translation of the Hungarian *Virag*, signifies, nevertheless, something living and unpretentiously pleasant. The name 'Leopold' derives from Old High German *Leutpald* or *Liutbald* and seems to signify that its owner is a man of the *liut* or *Leute* or *lewdie* – the people – but is distinguished by being *bald* or *bold*. Bloom's wife calls him Poldy, which ironically emphasises his boldness. In 'Circe' he becomes briefly Leo, but the leonine is not in his nature. His surname undergoes many mutations. Wind lengthens its vowel. When Joyce is trying to bring him and Stephen together, his name becomes 'Stoom' while Stephen's becomes 'Blephen', or it may be the other way about. In the report in the evening paper of Dignam's funeral, he is down as L. Boom (Stephen's name is there too, though he was not present; the man in the mackintosh is down as McIntosh). This deformation makes him explode into a (Dutch) tree; it can also be justified by the art of navigation which broods over the chapter. The joke is that, when Hynes collected the names that morning at Glasnevin, he took pains to get Bloom's first name right.

In the catechismal chapter, so that no reader may think that not all has been done that might have been done, we have the following:

What anagrams had he made on his name in youth?
Leopold Bloom.
Ellpodbomool.
Molldopeloob.
Bollopedoom
Old Ollebo, M.P.

What acrostic upon the abbreviation of his first name had he
(kinetic poet) sent to Miss Marion Tweedy on the 14 February
1888?

> Poets oft have sung in rhyme
> Of music sweet their praise divine.
> Let them hymn it nine times nine.
> Dearer far than song or wine,
> You are mine. The world is mine.

Bloom's middle name, which makes a shy and almost unnoticed
appearance, is Paula. All that need be said of this is that it links
his male and female natures, as also the Catholic world of his
mother and the Jewish one of his father. Miss Marion Tweedy's
name has its own symbolism. Being Cybele, a pagan earth-
mother, she has to be Christianised into the Virgin Mary
(whose birthday – September 8 – she shares), but *Mary* would
be both obvious and blasphemous. So '*Marion*', the old French
diminutive, must serve instead. As 'Molly', she is very nearly
predestined to be one flesh with Molldopeloob, and, in the
'Circe' episode, her name very nearly coincides with that of the
magical herb Odysseus was given by Hermes. Bloom really has
three kinds of moly (Hermes, after all, was god of the trivial
crossroads): his recent ejaculation, a flower which will protect
him from lust; the homely potato to keep off rheumatism, which
is at first mistaken by a whore for a hard chancre; and the
admonitory image of Molly herself. The surname 'Tweedy' is
highly appropriate for Penelope the weaver. *Tweed* was originally
a trademark, a misspelling – influenced by the river – of *tweel* or
tweeled, both Scottish variants of *twill*. Anglo-Saxon *twilic*, from
which *twill* derives, means 'two-threaded'. Molly has two kinds
of blood in her – Spanish and Irish.

The barmaids of 'Sirens' are, as I have already mentioned,
named for musical terms. Mina Purefoy, the tholing mother of
'Oxen of the Sun', keeps the pure ancient faith in fertility; her

husband, Theodore, sees children as God's gifts. Of the three whores in 'Circe', Zoe stands for the animal kingdom, though it is Florry – who stands for the vegetable – who has a stye in her eye. Kitty (Catherine) should evoke minerals, but she is merely – perhaps minerally – pure. Three men in the book – Rumbold the hangman, Private Compton and Private Carr – are named after old enemies of Joyce: the British Consul-General at Zurich in World War I, and two of his attachés. The story of Joyce's part in the production of *The Importance of Being Earnest* (intended as British propaganda in a neutral country), and the débâcle over a pair of trousers bought by Joyce for the play which the Consulate would not reimburse him for, and his eventual letter of complaint to His Majesty King George V, makes engrossing reading and may be read at length in Richard Ellmann's biography. Joyce was trying to be like Blake, who similarly put hated names in his Prophetic Books, though these were originally soldiers' names. Here is one of them, now a disembodied power of treachery: 'Go thou to Scofield: ask him whether he is Bath or Canterbury.' Other true names in *Ulysses* are attached to their historical owners – like Eglinton, Best and George Russell. Russell is also A.E., enabling Stephen, who is in his debt, to say to himself: 'A.E.I.O.U.' One great Dublin name walks through the streets with an apostrophe S that is always becoming detached: H.E.L.Y.S. Joyce's love of letters (being a man of them, he was forced to become that) here fuses with his love of names. He is never happier than when he can adorn a name with a comet-tail of letters, some of them obscene, as with (at the end of 'Cyclops') 'H.R.H., rear admiral the right honourable sir Hercules Hannibal Habeas Corpus Anderson K.G., K.P., K.T., P.C., K.C.B., M.P., J.P., M.B., D.S.O., S.O.D., M.F.H., M.R.I.A., B.L., Mus. Doc., P.L.G., F.T.C.D., F.R.U.I., F.R.C.P.I., and F.R.C.S.I.'

In this same chapter Joyce reveals himself as a great creator of comic names in the English tradition. The execution scene contains the following catalogue:

The delegation, present in full force, consisted of Commendatore Bacibaci Beninobenone (the semi-paralysed *doyen* of the party who had to be assisted to his seat by the aid of a powerful steam crane), Monsieur Pierrepaul Petitépatant, the Grandjoker Vladinmire Pokett-hankerscheff, the Archjoker Leopold Rudolph von Schwanzenbad-Hodenthaler, Countess Marha Virága Kisászony Putrápesthi, Hiram

Y. Bomboost, Count Athanatos Karamelopulos, Ali Baba Backsheesh Rahat Lokum Effendi, Señor Hidalgo Caballero Don Pecadillo y Palabras y Paternoster de la Malora de la Malaria, Hokopoko Harakiri, Hi Hung Chang, Olaf Kobberkeddelsen, Mynheer Trik van Trumps, Pan Poleaxe Paddyrisky, Goosepond Prhklstr Kratchinabritchisitch, Herr Hurhausdirektorpräsident Hans Chuechli-Steuerli, Nationalgymnasiummuseumsanatoriumandsuspensoriumsordinaryprivatdocentgeneralhistoryspecialprofessordoctor Kriegfried Ueberallgemein.

And the list of guests at the 'wedding of the chevalier Jean Wyse de Neulan, grand high chief ranger of the Irish National Foresters, with Miss Fir Conifer of Pine Valley' is delicious, even if it goes on too long. It is in such onomastic joy that Joyce seems already to be anticipating the mad namecalling of *Finnegans Wake*.

It depends, of course, on what one means by *mad*. In trying to discover what are the true names of some of the characters, why they are called what they are called, and why they sometimes change without warning, madness is the state of mind the reader frequently feels, but it is probable that Joyce always knows what he is doing, or thinks he knows. The dreamer of the dream which is *Finnegans Wake* is apparently, in his waking life, a Mr Porter. The name is appropriate for an innkeeper who sells stout, carries crates of it up from the cellar, bears a burden of sin, and transmits that burden along with the 'crossmess parzle' of life. His wife's name is certainly Ann, as his children's names are certainly Kevin, Jerry and Isobel. The cleaningwoman is Kate, though – because Joyce is fond of his parody of the song sung by the Bohea brothers in *Ulysses*: 'Summon in the housesweep Dina' – she is often called Dina. The cellarman's name is uncertain – sometimes Behan, sometimes Sackerson, sometimes Saunderson, sometimes plain Joe or Jo ('Poor old Joe' is his Fosterian refrain). As we meet these characters only in dream, it is probably pointless to discuss their waking names, but Joyce grants us a brief image (seen through the eyes of another dreamer) of the Porter family awaking, and there we feel impelled to grasp at what daylit fact we can. The sleeping name of Porter is, as we know, Humphrey Chimpden Earwicker. One of his real-life near-homonyms was the Victorian statesman Hugh Culling Eardley Childers, who was known in parliament as 'Here Comes Everybody' – a nickname borrowed for Earwicker, who is also called 'Haveth Childers Everywhere'. But the great dream-name itself seems to be cunningly constructed so as to suggest symbols without wholly revealing them. The name 'Earwicker' does not seem to exist in real life. I have made it a hobby to look for it in the telephone directories of all the towns I visit, but I have not yet found it, though *Earwaker* is often there – six times, as I remember in the London directory. William York Tindall suggests that 'Earwicker' is meant to sound Scandinavian – appropriately, as Earwicker is, among other things, one of the Scandinavian invaders of Dublin – and that it contains a metathetised *era* for time and a *wick* for place. '*Wick*' properly means a village or town and it is derived ultimately from Latin '*vicus*', a form which became '*vico*' in Italian and is the name of the presiding historiographer of the *Wake* – Giovanni Battista Vico (1668–1744), whose doctrine of the historical cycle gives the book a shape analogous to that provided by the Odyssey in the other book.

'Earwicker', suggesting *earwig*, is also a begetter of symbolic entomology. This middleaged father, no longer sexually attracted to his wife, feels carnal desire for his daughter and, one thinks, also for his son Kevin, but his dream is unwilling to present him with the dreaded word *incest*. This has to be metathetised to *insect*, which encourages the dermapteral to crawl out of his surname to such an extent that this Protestant Nordic innkeeper can present himself as the Irish patriot Persse O'Reilly. This is, of course, the French *perce-oreille*, meaning *earwig*. The first name 'Humphrey' suggests the load of guilt Earwicker carries on his back, as well as the hump of the egg which, though it has a dump as well, is a symbol of new life: sin and creation are inseparable. 'Chimpden' turns him into *Pan troglodytes*, shoving him underground for his excessive animality. Needless to say, none of these interpretations tell the entire story, nor should they: if a dream could be totally explained it would not be a dream, and this applies to the names in it. Most of Earwicker's other names, of which there are many, are fanciful but appropriate fillings out of his initials.

Ann Porter is mostly Anna Livia Plurabelle – the river Liffey with its many beauties – but her name is capable of transformation to such forms as 'Annushka Lutetiavitch Pufflovah'. She is all rivers and she can be traced ultimately to a source in Russia; why else does she address her waking child as 'Muy malinchily malchick!', which can be my 'My cold and melancholy male chick' but is essentially Russian for 'my little boy' – '*moiy malyenki malchik*'? Her daughter Isobel or Izzy is often Iseult la Belle, which fits well into one of the mythic layers of the book but is also highly proper for a girl born in Chapelizod – the chapel of Izod or Iseult of the White Hands (not the one with whom Tristram primarily fell in love but the one he eventually married: in the dream they become, inevitably, confused). Jerry and Kevin we meet mostly as Shem and Shaun, names Joyce took from a pair of inseparable and idiotic Dublin brothers. They have, however, a very privy significance in terms of Joyce's own family. Shem is James and Shaun is John. James Joyce as a boy was called 'Sunny Jim', while his brother Stanislaus, sterner but always more reliable, was termed 'Brother John'. The opposed elements James saw in Stanislaus and himself, especially when they were living together in Trieste, have been mythicised and eternised in the twin warring sons of Earwicker. They have other names too. Shaun turns himself into Jaun, a liverish lover of ladies; Haun, a barnyard strutter (German *Hahn*); Yawn, a huge hill of emptiness. Shem and Shaun become a stem and a stone, the one a source of life, the other a dead lump. They are Chuff and Glugg or Nick and Mick (Old Nick and the Archangel Michael) or Dolph and Kev or Tristopher and Hilary (the sad one and the gay one). Their respective functions in life are clarified in the names 'Shem the Penman' and 'Shaun the Post': the one creates the Word, the other only delivers it (and then in a debased form).

The four old men who, with the Twelve and the Twenty-eight (or nine), perform subsidiary roles in the nightlong drama, have the names Matthew Gregory, Mark Lyons, Luke Tarpey and Johnny MacDougal. They represent the four provinces of Ireland and also the four gospellers. Fused into one, they become Mamalujo. The Twelve are either members of the Sullivan clan or the Doyle, but – as with the month-of-February girls of St Bride's – their individual names count for little. It is number that makes for identity, fulfilling the law of the Cabbala. The onomastics of *Finnegans Wake* is hardly separable from the study of its entire structure and texture: the whole work is a monstrous act of naming. The name of the book itself is a clue to Joyce's technique. *Finnegans Wake*, as a title, is not to be confused with 'Finnegan's Wake', which is the name of the New York Irish ballad which was one of Joyce's primary inspirations. 'Finne-

gan's Wake' is about the fall of Tim Finnegan, a drunken bricklayer, from his ladder at work, and the drunken lamentations
which honour his corpse. There is a fight, and whisky is spilt
on him; whereupon he wakes, crying: 'Whirl your liquor around
like blazes – Souls to the devil! D'ye think I'm dead?' This is
good demotic resurrection myth and a very useful groundbass
for Joyce's essentially (despite everything) demotic book.
Finnegans Wake, as a title, contains the name of the song, but it
contains, in addition, two opposed notions jammed together in
'*Finnegans*' – the end (*fin*) and the resumption (*again*) – as well as
in '*Wake*' (a funeral celebration and a rising again). The death-
and-resurrection process is timeless and universal: all kinds of
Finnegans perform the act of waking. At certain points in history
it seems that we have come to an impasse, so that the end says
no to the possibility of starting again – '*Fin negans Wake*'. In our
own debased age we are swimming in the wake of departed
heroism. And so on. I have already, I see, entered on to an
explication of Joyce's punning technique, and we had better
start examining this technique at length and in earnest.

It remains, though, to say something about the names in Joyce's
own life. He took seriously the business of the appositeness of a
name to its owner, as did his father who, hearing that he had
run away with a girl named Nora Barnacle, prophesied that she
would cling to him for ever. It worried Joyce that Swift should
not be Sterne and Sterne Swift. Harriet Shaw Weaver, his patron-
ess, had a name of good omen: she was a faithful Penelope who
gave freely and demanded of him only that he be faithful to his
work. Joyce thought that his own name had the same derivation
as Freud's, so that he was as authentic and authoritative an
analyst of the soul. To James Stephens, who had his own first
name and that of his autobiographical hero, and additionally
shared a birthday with him, he was prepared at one point to
hand over the labour of completing *Finnegans Wake*. When the
second world war began and the Finns fought back bravely at the
Russians, he half-believed that their heroism derived from their
name. (Nora Barnacle, incidentally, was predestined to be the
wife of the author of the *Wake*, since she had worked at Finn's
Hotel). Cheerfully slavish to a homemade doctrine of word-
magic and an ingenious capacity for false etymology, he wove such
names as had no magic of their own into *Finnegans Wake* and con-

ferred magic on them there. Mr Knight, manager of the Euston
Hotel in London and a 'very knice kman', becomes 'Knight,
tuntapster', just as Gorman, author of his first biography, is
fixed among the timeless 'hagiographers'. Mulligan calls Stephen
'Kinch' because the sound is that of a knifeblade. Long long
after June 16, 1904, a shopkeeper called Kinch set himself up on
the road from Dublin to the Sandycove tower. Needless to say,
he knows nothing about Joyce.

CHAPTER 10

Oneiroparonomastics

BEFORE Joyce – or, strictly, before Lewis Carroll – a pun was mainly a humorous, often childishly humorous, word-trick involving the exploitation of homophones or homonyms. Victorian burlesque-writers, many of whom were contributors to *Punch*, brought the trick very low, but there had been a time when the pun could serve as serious an end as the riddle. The Delphic oracle, telling a general both to stay at home and not to stay at home, employed a pun: *Domine, stes* sounds the same as *Domi ne stes*. The enquirer took the latter meaning, went out to battle and was killed. Lady Macbeth proposes to gild the faces of the groom with King Duncan's blood to make it seem their guilt. Bahram the great hunter was, says Omar Khayyam, always hunting *gur* (wild asses), but now the *gur* (grave) has hunted him down. As Joyce was always telling his friends, the Christian Church was founded on a pun. He himself, as was to be expected, rejoyced in little puns. He had a view of Cork framed in cork. Leaving a tea-party in Paris he thanked his host thus: '*Je vous remercie de votre bonté et de votre bon thé.*' But the kind of paronomasia he was eventually to specialise in went much further than that. The term *pun* will not really do for the word-play of *Finnegans Wake*. We need a word like – let us go further: we need the word itself – *jabberwocky*. Strangely enough, Joyce had not read either of the *Alice* books when he began to publish sections of *Work in Progress* (the name given to *Finnegans Wake* when it was merely work in progress), but, having read them, he was quick to see in Lewis Carroll himself an avatar of Earwicker, and when, in the waking section of the *Wake*, Ann Porter soothes her child out of a nightmare, she says ''Tis jest jibberweek's joke' – a reassurance which may be meant for the reader who has come so far, not just for crying Kevin.

Jabberwocky is a fantastic extension of the pun, suitable for depicting the matter of dreams or hallucination, which frequently take an ambiguous or multiguous view of the material provided by waking experience. The coat of arms of the Shakespeare family, which shows as its crest an eagle shaking a spear, is a kind of pun weakened by etymology, but when Joyce calls Shakespeare – very justly – 'Shapesphere' he has gone a step further than homophony or homonymy. By changing two consonants he has interfered minimally with the shape of the name and enormously expanded its connotation. This sort of minimal mutation is common enough in traditional punning. In *Alice in Wonderland* we tremble on the brink of something bigger. A school of fishes becomes a real school by the dream-law which takes homonymous puns not as jokes but as statements of double fact, and all that follows has to confirm the duality. There are not enough homonyms or homophones in the language to make further puns of the *school* variety, so we have to have 'reeling, writhing and fainting in coils' (the first two good, the third a little forced). When, as in *Through the Looking Glass*, a dream-word seems to have no primary or radical meaning, but is apparently compounded of two or more meanings that subsist on the same level of importance, then we are, literally, in the sphere of Jabberwocky. It is easy to see that in 'reeling' the radical meaning is *reading*, but it is not possible to say whether, in 'slithy', *slimy* or *lithe* comes first, or whether, in 'gimble', *gambol* (with *tumble* behind it) precedes the *gimlet* element. Humpty Dumpty calls these 'portmanteau words' and is an admirable exegetist of them. It is this type of word that Joyce uses, though he crams the portmanteau sometimes to bursting, with elements taken from foreign languages as well as English.

When part of *Work in Progress* appeared as the Faber pamphlet *Haveth Childers Everywhere*, Joyce wrote an advertisement for it:

> Humptydump Dublin squeaks through his norse,
> Humptydump Dublin hath a horrible vorse
> And with all his kinks english
> Plus his irismanx brogues
> Humptydump Dublin's grandada of all rogues.

This relates the great difficult book to a charming one for children, and it presents the language as not very formidable. For *Anna*

Livia Plurabelle he contrived an equally disarming puff, or Pufflo-vah:

> Buy a book in brown paper
> From Faber & Faber
> To see Annie Liffey trip, tumble and caper.
> Sevensinns in her singthings,
> Plurabelle on her prose,
> Seashell ebb music wayriver she flows.

The promoters took fright, nevertheless, and the plurabelle prose came out without Joyce's charming advocacy. But he used the *Wake* style in a composition which got into the *New Statesman and Nation* and the American *Hound and Horn* in 1932 – an article called 'From a Banned Writer to a Banned Singer'. The singer was the Irish-French tenor John Sullivan who, Joyce was convinced, had received less than his due from the world of musical promotion. Sullivan's voice, as the singer himself admitted, was past its best at that time, but Joyce stubbornly heard only its original vigour and its phenomenal range. As he was concerned not with stunning his readers with difficulties but wooing them into taking Sullivan's voice at his, the banned writer's, evaluation, the propaganda he wrote had to be fresh, humorous, ingenious but not obscure. As it stands, it is an admirable way into the difficulties of the *Wake*:

Just out of kerryosity howlike is a Sullivan? It has the fortefaccia of a Markus Brutas, the wingthud of a spreadeagle, the body uniformed of a metropoliceman with the brass feet of a collared grand. It cresces up in Aquilone but diminuends austrowards. It was last seen and heard of by some macgillicuddies above a lonely valley of their reeks, dustening the greylight as it flew, its cry echechohoing among the anfractuosities: *pour la dernière fois*. The blackbulled ones, stampeding, drew in their horns, all appailed and much upset, which explains the guttermilk on their overcoats.

This, in its simple way, exhibits clearly enough the potentialities of Joyce's newspeak. 'Kerryosity' is primarily *curiosity*, but it also tells us that Sullivan comes from Kerry, land of the mountains known as Macgillicuddy's Reeks. 'Howlike' seems not very complimentary, but it places Sullivan among the great loud piercing voices of nature. 'A Sullivan' turns him into a large monster or astonishing phenomenon; at the same time it personifies the voice, which matters more than the man. The 'fortefaccia' is not a true Italian word, but it conveys the strength of the impact made by the voice and it contains a wide-ranging musical phrase – F E F A C C A – suitable for it. The voice is as grand as imperial Rome: the 'spreadeagle' provides an enharmonic chord which modulates from natural power to the power of human organisation; it is also a minor example of the way in which Joyce can revive the original strength of a tired metaphor. 'Wingthud' is the kind of economical compound of which Joyce is fond in *Ulysses* – admirable and inevitable once we have met it, not at all bizarre or forced. The voice has the bulk and authority of a policeman and it is apt for the Metropolitan Opera; its deeper notes have the holding power of the feet of a Collard grand piano. The notes produced in the nasopharynx sweep as high as an eagle (Sullivan also, apparently, had an aquiline nose). 'Echechohoing' is an example of the way in which the author will force a conventional semanteme into being iconic; it also introduces Earwicker's own musical phrase, crabbed into E C H, H being the German for B natural. '*Pour la dernière fois*' comes from the French version of *William Tell*, in which, according to Joyce, Sullivan could be superb; Sullivan's last visit to Ireland (recent when the article was written) is paralleled by Arnold's last visit, in the opera, to his mountain home. And so on. There are references which are either self-explanatory or else not explanatory at all, unless one possesses information which only the author and his subject have and hug to themselves. The real problems of *Finnegans Wake* are not semantic but referential. Joyce loves to mystify, and the mysteries yield less to the language scholar than to the diligent enquirer into the facts of Joyce's life, or the lives of his friends.

This *jeu d'esprit* in dead, or living, earnest has nothing to do with dreams, except with the unrealised ones of Sullivan's professional success. The language of *Finnegans Wake*, on the other hand, justifies its difficulties and unprecedented complexities in terms of its subject-matter. Joyce, having exhausted the potentialities of waking English in *Ulysses*, was compelled, in his next book, to 'put the language to sleep'. Freed by sleep of the rigidities of daytime modes of interpreting time and space, language becomes fluid. Opening itself up to the incursions of images from man's collective unconscious, it is also willing to be fertilised by many of the other languages of the world. Many, but not all. The dream is to be about human history, but only that segment which has relevance to a Western brain sleeping in a Western bed. China and Japan and the East Indies do not submit their languages for inclusion in the huge dialect, except in the debased, Westernised, forms of pidgin. The sleeper, a publican in Chapelizod, a suburb of Dublin south-west of Phoenix Park, turns himself into Universal Man, but Universal Man schooled mainly in the Indo-European languages, especially Dublin English. He re-enacts, in a single night's sleep, the essential movements of Western history, using his own family and the customers of his pub as an acting troupe which must take on many roles: he himself plays all the heavy leads. The history presented is not what we learned at school, a treadmill of dates and dynasties and battles. The Italian philosopher Vico provides a cyclical view of history, seeing it all as an ever-revolving wheel with four segments chalked on its felloe (felloe = fellow = man; I do not think Joyce thought of this pun). Each segment represents a historical phase. First, there is fabulous prehistory, when men worship gods and pay heed to their words, expressed in thunder; next, there is a period of aristocratic rule – patriarchal as opposed to theocratic; next, there is a debasement of the aristocratic principle, in which demos is led by windy demagogues; then human society sinks to a hopeless state of chaos, so that, to be redeemed, man must once more listen to the thunder, pay heed to the gods, and see the wheel start a new revolution. The god-hero Finn MacCool represents the first phase in Joyce's version of Vico. He is followed by the patriarch, the good honest family man, whom Earwicker is qualified to play. But as there is only one actor, himself, capable of taking the heavy roles, he must enact Finn as well as his own part. Finn is humanised into Finnegan, the drunken bricklayer, but he is still the giant on whose stretched-out body the city of Dublin rests. Earwicker, as Earwicker, falls like Adam and is removed from the Edenborough he rules, to be replaced by his sons, one of whom is an artist unfitted for the postures of authority, while the other is a bloated travesty of the father he seeks to succeed. The general mess leads to a *ricorso* – Vico's term – in which the great father-figure is invoked, so that the phase of

theocratic rule can start the wheel turning again. The book itself
is circular in that it never comes to an end. The last word on the
last page is 'the', and this governs the first word – 'riverrun' – on
the first page.

   Armed with this basic information, it ought to be possible for
the average reader, whoever or whatever he is, to make a start
at cutting his way through the wiry heathpacks of language. He
may feel entitled to the help of a Virgilian guide equipped with
special training and insight, but each of us is really on his own.
If I, who am a kind of shadowy guide, presume to help the
stumbler, this does not signify that I myself am immune from
stumbling. Let us take some of the enigmas of the prelude, which
contains many of the themes to be developed in the pages that
follow.

Sir Tristram, violer d'amores, fr'over the short sea, had passencore
rearrived from North Armorica on this side the scraggy isthmus of
Europe Minor to wielderfight his penisolate war . . .

At the beginning of the story of the *Wake*, certain events – those
belonging to the later phases of the cycle but not to the theocratic
phase – have not yet happened; but, because history is a wheel, we
know that they are going to happen: indeed, since the cycle
presents an *éternel retour*, they have happened before, though not
in any age of gods and heroes. The verb 'rearrived' makes the
repetitive element clear. Sir Tristram is the Tristram of Arthurian
legend but also the Sir Almeric Tristram who founded the St
Lawrence family and built Howth Castle. He is a violator of
Iseult, of his own honour, and of the marital rights of his uncle
King Mark. Mark must be Earwicker, Iseult his own daughter,
and Tristram one or the other of his twin sons. The 'violer
d'amores' refers also to the instrument called a viola d'amore,
found in baroque orchestras, but associated here with courtly
love and troubadours. The instrument has seven strings, which
relates it to rainbows. We shall meet rainbows later and see why
they are important in the *Wake*. North Armorica is both America
and Brittany: what happens in the Old World also happens in
the New, which may be regarded as a spatial representation of a
renewed cycle – diachronic as synchronic. If there is a King Mark
in the Old World, we shall not be surprised to find a Mark II,
or Mark Twain, in the New, complete with two boys (one of

them a Finn) to show that he is really HCE. The passage contains
two foreign importations – the French *pas encore* – 'not yet' –
as 'passencore' and the German *wieder* – 'again' – in 'wielderfight'. The first is no very useful coinage, though it points at the
language of Armorica, where – as a Celtic tongue also is spoken –
there is a confluence or conflict of different cultures as in Dublin
itself. It also suggests *passion* and *coeur* as well as *passenger*. *Wieder*
emphasises the recurrence of 'wielding weapons in wild fight'.
'Fr'over' is both a suitable archaism and a word that adds the
colour of *rover* to Tristram's passionate passage. 'Penisolate war'
is primarily the Peninsular War of Napoleon and Wellington –
parts which warring brothers are qualified to play – and it contains ambiguous connotations which make it impossible for us to
decide, at this stage, which of the twins will be playing Tristram.
For 'penisolate' can mean 'with pen in isolation', proper for the
exiled, silent and cunning Shem the penman, or else 'waged of
late with the penis', applicable to Shaun-Jaun, whose eroticism
may be taken as a matter of recent, or current, history. Joyce is
clear on one point in the *Wake*, and that is that our own age is
debased and is due for a *ricorso*.

... nor avoice from afire bellowsed mishe mishe to tauftauf thuart-
peatrick ...

The peat-rick is Ireland herself. Two Irish legends are conjoined
in a fiery image (hell, St Patrick's Purgatory, the flames of divine
oracle, as in the parted tongues of the pentecostal paraclete).
'Mishe mishe' – Irish for 'I am, I am' – is associated with St
Bridget, who heard the voice of God uttering the *Om* which is
missing from Sir Tristram's 'fr'over'. St Patrick's tutor was St
Germanicus, so it is dreamily appropriate that *baptise* should appear
as 'tauftauf' (German *taufen*), especially as this points the factor
of importation common to both Ireland's religion and the pre-
republic Irish state, as well as suggesting the continuity and
supranational essence of Christian evangelism. Later in the book,
'tauftauf' becomes a nickname – 'Toffy Tough' – and finally,
which is fitting for baptism, 'douche douche'. This is a fair
example of Joyce's progressive punning. First he changes by
ablaut, later by a consonantal shift within the initial area (/t/ to
/d/ – unvoiced stop to its voiced partner; /f/ to /ʃ/ – one unvoiced

fricative to another). 'Douche douche' is also a portmanteau: it echoes 'mishe mishe'.

... not yet, though venissoon after, had a kidscad buttended a bland old isaac; not yet, though all's fair in vanessy, were sosie sesthers wroth with twone nathandjoe.

Both 'venissoon' and 'vanessy' may suggest Inverness which, with the 'sesthers', may call up a dim image of Macbeth and Banquo meeting the witches who promise the rule of Scotland to both their houses. The 'fair' points two ways – to 'all's fair in love and war', a very apt proverb for the twin brothers, and to 'so fair and foul a day'. Shem appears later as 'Lack breath' who shall 'leap no more', so he may take the main part here. 'Venisoon' is 'very soon' with a strong whiff of venison, redolent of Old Testament sacrifices. Jacob, who is also James or Giacomo or Shem, showed artist's cunning in disguising himself – the cadet of the brothers, but also the cad – as Shaun-Esau by means of a kidskin, thus duping his bland-blind old father Isaac into giving him his blessing. Here is Isaac Butt as well, Hibernicising the Bible as the Irish Nationalist leader whom Parnell ousted. In the references that follow we shift to another part of the old Testament, picking out Susanna, Esther and Ruth – girls loved by older men – as well as Nathan and Joseph. These last two – the wise prophet and the hero who would not yield to the unlawful importunities of Zuleika, Potiphar's wife – are joined to contain an anagram of the first name of Swift, Dean of St Patrick's. He, Nathan and Joe in one – 'twone', earned the wrath of the two Esthers in his life, Esther Johnson (Stella) and Esther Van-homrigh (Vanessa), for failing to respond adequately to their love for him. This is evidently a part for Earwicker, tempted and resisting father, though not in God. The two Esthers appear as 'sosies', doubles of each other (French *sosie*, from the classical *Sosia*, a character in Plautus, who loved mistaken identities), and for a reason pretty obvious when we remember that the Porter troupe contains only one nubile girl. Isobel has a habit of talking to her own reflection in the mirror, and Joyce makes the mirror-image come to life when she has to play sosial parts (the two girls in the Phoenix Park, for instance, or the colleens who are the supporters of the Dublin coat of arms). It is in such a seemingly artificial device that Joyce discloses one of the touching family realities that underlie the whole fantasy of the *Wake* and make it a living personal document. His own daughter Lucia is still living out a schizophrenic existence in a sanatorium in England.

Rot a peck of pa's malt had Jhem or Shen brewed by arclight and rory end to the regginbrow was to be seen ringsome on the aquaface.

Here is an important biblical motif in a book with so much drinking in it. Noah, who is a family man like Earwicker and a sort of winegod like Finnegan, learned how to brew after the flood and passed on the secret to his sons, our fathers. The rainbow – 'heptarch' or *arc-en-ciel* or *Regenbogen* – spanned the heavens as a covenant, seven colours matched by the seven strings of the viola d'amore, an emblem of hope to contrast with the thunder, God's warning. The rainbow comes and goes throughout the *Wake*, often mimed by the twenty-eight girls of St Bride's Academy (which is Ireland), who are divided by four for the purpose. The brothers Shem and Shaun have here to take on three roles – Shem, Ham and Japhet – but Joyce contents himself with a kind of onomastic impressionism. Latinate and Germanic verbal elements are well balanced in this passage: 'rot' for *red*, 'rory' for *dew*, 'ringsome' (*ringsum*) for 'in the manner of a circle, like the *Wake* itself', and so on.

Our understanding of Joyce's jabberwocky depends, as may now be dimly apparent, on other factors than a linguistic ingenuity that matches the author's own. There has to be curious learning – encyclopaedic rather than mere lexicographical knowledge – and much of it must seem wanton, cranky and useless. But Joyce's aim is to draw from history those factors which best confirm the universality of his myth. 'The fall,' he says, 'of a once wallstrait oldparr is retaled early in bed and later on life down through all christian minstrelsy.' As we are concerned with the world-shattering fall of a god, the 1930 'wallstrait' crash may seem relevant, but why 'oldparr'? A parr is a young salmon; the salmon is Finn MacCool's totem. Old Parr was the oldest man who ever lived, guilty of begetting bastards in his hundred-and-fiftieth year. 'Bygmester Finnegan, of the Stuttering Hand, freemen's maurer' is described as 'oftwhile balbulous'. If we remember that Finnegan (or Finn) and HCE are, for all practical purposes, the same man, that 'Bygmester' will make total sense. It is Dano-Norwegian for *masterbuilder*, but it is one

particular Masterbuilder who is referred to – Ibsen's Halvard
Solness, who has built a tower at the request of a young woman he
loves, climbs it and falls from it, figuratively struck down by the
God he seems to attempt to rival. HCE is guiltily in love with his
own daughter, and the guilt comes out in a stutter – hence the
'Stuttering Hand', a transference which is, in its quiet way,
potent. 'Balbulous' refers to Balbus, who was always building a
wall, but the term means 'stutterer'. The tremor of guilt is
transformed into a creative act. Man was thrust out of Eden to
build his own substitute for it – the city. Without sin there is no
creativity, no history. The dynamo that powers the wheel,
stuttering and shuddering with energy, is original sin. A guilty
erection leads to a glorious erection. We are free, despite the
tendency to sin, and freedom is best manifested in the creative
act. Every great man is a 'freeman's maurer'. If Joyce had lived,
he would have made something out of the shameful *Mauer* that
divides Berlin, seeing it as a debased act of building appropriate
to the age of the warring brothers. Everything can be made to
fit the mythology of the *Wake*, even the sound of the nuclear
bomb.

The most spectacular of Joyce's portmanteaux are the hundred-
letter words which stand for thunder – loud enough for a thermo-
dynamic explosion, quiet enough for the collapse of a reputation.
To copy examples out is a headaching business, for typist and
printer alike, and I will content myself with two. Most readers
skip them, taking in the visual configuration and ignoring the
onomatopoeia, but those who wish to read Joyce aloud should
try arranging the syllables in a kind of verse-pattern, as with this
on the first page of the book:

bababad-	7
algharagh-	9
takamminar-	10
ronnkonn-	8
bronntonnerronn-	15
tuonnthunn-	10
trovarrhounawn-	14
skawn-	5
toohoohoorden-	13
enthurnuk!	9
	100

This is evidently the thunder announcing, in various languages, its thundery essence. Here HCE in fatherly anger, slams the door:

Lukkedoeren-	11
dunandurra-	10
skewdylooshoo-	13
fermoyporter-	12
tooryzooy-	9
sphalnabortans-	14
porthao-	7
kansakroid-	10
verjkapak-	9
kapuk.	5
	100

It is the cold care of the addition which is somehow shocking, disclosing as it does the engineering which lies behind the dream. The successive drafts of the *Wake* similarly remind us how unspontaneous the whole structure is, despite the appearance of mad abandon. Here, for instance, is the first version of part of the 'Anna Livia Plurabelle' chapter, as published in 1925 in the periodical *Navire d'Argent*:

Tell me, tell me, how could she cam through all her fellows, the daredevil? Linking one and knocking the next and polling in and petering out and clyding by in the eastway. Who was the first that ever burst? Someone it was, whoever you are. Tinker, tailor, soldier, sailor, Paul Pry or polishman.

Two years later, in *transition*, it had become:

Tell me, tell me, how could she cam through all her fellows, the neckar she was, the diveline? Linking one and knocking the next, tapping a flank and tipping a jutty and palling in and petering out and clyding by on her eastway. Wai-whou was the first that ever burst? Someone he was, whoever they were, in a tactic attack or in single combat. Tinker, tailor, soldier, sailor, Paul Pry or polishman. That's the thing I always want to know.

The following year it has been inspissated to this:

Tell me, tell me, how cam she camlin through all her fellows, the neckar she was, the diveline? Linking one and knocking the next, tapting a flank and tipting a jutty and palling in and pietaring out and clyding by on her eastway. Waiwhou was the first thurever burst?

Someone he was, whuebra they were, in a tactic attack or in single combat. Tinker, tilar, souldrer, salor, Pieman Peace or Polistamann. That's the thing I always want to know.

In the final version, the one incorporated in the book itself, it is thicker still. One cannot say as thick as possible, since Joyce, had he lived to prepare a second edition, would undoubtedly have gone further:

Tell me, tell me, how cam she camlin through all her fellows, the neckar she was, the diveline? Casting her perils before our swains from Fonte-in-Monte to Tidingtown and from Tidingtown tilhavet. Linking one and knocking the next, tapting a flank and tipting a jutty and palling in and pietaring out and clyding by on her eastway. Wai-whou was the first thurever burst? Someone he was, whuebra they were, in a tactic attack or in single combat. Tinker, tilar, souldrer, salor, Pieman Peace or Polistaman. That's the thing I'm elwys on edge to esk.

He might, for instance, have changed 'in a tactic attack or in single combat', which is painfully naked, to something like 'inner stackstick tattack or in sinful wombat'.

The piling on of extra connotations is of the essence of the palimpsestuous – or palincestuous – technique. Joyce celebrates Anna Livia as not only Dublin's river but all rivers, and he crams the text with the names of all the rivers that fit, without overmuch straining, into a dream-washerwoman's idiolect. This ingenuity, which impresses the reader less than it seems to have impressed the author, is only accidentally justified: it blurs the sound and suggests vague crepuscular extra meanings which it is not important to pursue. If 'That's the thing I'm elwys on edge to esk' is better than 'That's the thing I always want to know', it is because it could only belong to a dream, whereas the other is essentially a waking kind of statement. One of the lessons to be learnt from comparing the various drafts is that we can be fairly happy with the fairly unintelligible. The triumph of much of the *Wake* is a prosodic triumph, in which rhythm, jingle and reduplication seem to tell us about the essential nature of primitive speech, or speech dimly heard in the next room, or the babble of speech in a crowded pub – the kind of speech, in fact, which it is unprofitable to ana-lyse into the segments of a more 'meaningful' communication.

Nevertheless, many of Joyce's inventions can be netted from

the ever-flowing stream and examined, glittering, in the tank. I take, more or less at random, ten examples of his dream-wit and economy.

1. O foenix culprit!
2. Mildew Lisa.
3. Nolans Brumans.
4. Darkpark's acoo with sucking loves.
5. Swiney Tod, ye Diamon Barbar!
6. the bairdboard bombardment screen.
7. the abnihilisation of the etym.
8. mielodorous.
9. a baskerboy on the Libido.
10. our wholemole millwheeling vicociclometer.

'O foenix culprit!' Earwicker is guilty of a vague crime in the Phoenix Park. Joyce parodies St Augustine's '*O felix culpa*' – happy that sin of Adam which was to merit so great a redeemer. Out of sin comes creation. 'Mildew Lisa' is the nickname given to O'Mara, 'an exprivate secretary of no fixed abode', who is partly responsible for spreading slanders about HCE. The name is a deformation of '*Mild und leise*' – the opening words that Isolde (Iseult) sings over dead Tristan (Tristram) in Wagner's music drama. Even in a low Dublin context the serious theme of an ancient guilty love can be invoked. 'Nolans Brumans' is the verdict pronounced by the four old men (Matthew, Mark, Luke and John – Mamalujo or Mammon Lujius) in the trial of Shaun – a re-enactment of the trial of his father HCE. Shem, his twin, is the chief witness for the prosecution and his evidence is suspect. The judges invoke the doctrine of Giordano Bruno of Nola – called 'The Nolan' by Joyce in earlier writings – to the effect that all opposites, in a divinely governed universe, must cancel each other out. A pun of this kind is a useful shorthand for Joyce, and he is lucky to find it incarnated in the name of a Dublin publishing firm – Browne and Nolan – which he is not slow to draw into the fabric of the *Wake*.

'Darkpark's acoo with sucking loves.' The day is ended, the play of the children is over, and the Phoenix Park, near their home, comes alive with human turtle doves (the real ones in the Zoo are asleep). This is good plain Joyce, apt for *Ulysses*. The next statement is about God, seen by Shem in bloody sacrificial

terms (*Schweinstod* – pigsdeath). God is the demon barber of
Fleet Street fame, but he is also the father who looks down on
Stephen Dedalus in the cradle – 'with his broad and hairy face, to
Ireland a disgrace'. He is barbarous as well as literally bearded.
The next two specimens are curiously prophetic. Joyce did not
live in the television age, but he plants a television set in HCE's
dream-pub. Baird had already made his experiments, and it
seemed possible that his system might be the one to be generally
adopted. The description is vivid and suggestive even in waking
terms. The atom bomb, in No. 7, means not the end of things so
much as the creation of new forms, new meanings, out of nothing
– *ab nihilo*. Joyce is optimistic: 11 always follows 32. 'Mielodorous' is applied to Shaun the singing demagogue, apostrophised
as a songbird. He is melodious and he smells of honey; he also
stinks. No. 9 described the Ondt in Shaun's fable, enjoying the
'melody that mints the money. *Ad majorem l.s.d.*' It explains
itself and it is admirable. The final example describes the *Wake*
itself, or life as presented by the *Wake*. We ride the bicycle made
by Vico, we burrow in the dark; life is dark and hard, but we
do not lack bread.

These specimens indicate that the verbal techniques of the
Wake could lend themselves to exploitation in imaginative prose
dealing with the daytime world. But prose tradition rejects such
compression as it rejects the implied febrile state of so high-
pitched a narration. A deranged narrator, like those in Nabokov's
Lolita and *Pale Fire*, can be entrusted with coinages like these. If
the narrator is not deranged he had better be dreaming. This
brings us, by a very short cycle ride, back to *Finnegans Wake*. On
the other hand, wordplay of this kind is at least as intelligible
as some of the later verse of Shakespeare or the early verse of
Donne. Encouraged by this knowledge, the timid would-be
reader of the *Wake* may be prepared to find long stretches that
make something like sense. Like, for instance, this description
of the eating habits of Shem (really Joyce himself):

So low was he that he preferred Gibsen's teatime salmon tinned, as
inexpensive as pleasing, to the plumpest roeheavy lax or the friskiest
parr or smolt troutlet that ever was gaffed between Leixlip and Island
Bridge and many was the time he repeated in his botulism that no
junglegrown pineapple ever smacked like the whoppers you shook out
of Ananias' cans, Findlater and Gladstone's, Corner House, England.

None of your inchthick blueblooded Balaclava fried-at-belief-stakes or juicejelly legs of the Grex's molten mutton or greasilygristly grunters' goupons or slice upon slab of luscious goosebosom with lump after load of plumpudding stuffing all aswim in a swamp of bogoakgravy . . .

What the innocent reader will worry about is not the vocabulary but the conjoined preoccupations. Why this emphasis on food – and, indeed, the book is crammed with it like a nightmare supermarket – and why bring in lies and martyrdom? We have already met *parr* and know that the salmon is Finn's own fish. Shem rejects it fresh and pure, therefore he rejects Finn, therefore he rejects Ireland. He prefers the false to the true, and this turns ananas (pineapple) into Ananias. He lacks patriotic conviction and would not go to the stake for his beliefs. He does not like to belong to the grex or sheep-flock. Shem's 'lowness' is expressed in terms of food because it is a sacramental duty to eat the dead god Finnegan and it is a filial right to consume the substance of the dead father HCE. The exiled artist rejects both the right and the duty.

Very occasionally the language of the *Wake* thrusts off the blanket of the dark and seems to have nothing sleepy about it:

Honuphrius is a concupiscent exservicemajor who makes dishonest propositions to all. He is considered to have committed, invoking *droit d'oreiller*, simple infidelities with Felicia, a virgin, and to be practising for unnatural coits with Eugenius and Jeremias, two or three philadelphians. Honuphrius, Felicia, Eugenius and Jeremias are consanguineous to the lowest degree. Anita the wife of Honuphrius has been told by her tirewoman, Fortissa, that Honuphrius has blasphemously confessed under voluntary chastisement that he has instructed his slave, Mauritius, to urge Magravius, a commercial, emulous of Honuphrius, to solicit the chastity of Anita.

This parody of Bayle comes from the *Ricorso*, where the corruption of our world has to be examined. Joyce disguises HCE as Honuphrius, his wife as Anita, and his sons as Eugenius and Jeremias, and weaves a tissue of total sexual depravity the more disgusting for being couched in cold legalistic language. But how can the undreamlike quality of the prose be justified if the dream is still proceeding? Some commentators have assumed that, as we have seen the Porters waking and getting out of bed before getting back into it, we are totally, if temporally, outside the world of dreams, but this is not so. The bigger dream which encloses that of Porter-Earwicker goes on, dreamed by Joyce or Finnegan or Finnegan-Joyce. The legal question arising out of the above statement is: has Honuphrius hegemony and shall Anita submit? The legal answer is: 'so long as there is a joint deposit account in the two names a mutual obligation is posited.' We then discuss a bad cheque:

... a good washable pink, embossed D you D No 11 hundred and thirty 2, good for the figure and face, had been circulating in the country for over thirtynine years among holders of Pango stock ... though not one demonetised farthing had ever spun or fluctuated across the counter in the semblance of hard coin or liquid cash.

Joyce is hitting at the Church of England (to which the Porters belong). The thirty-nine years stand for the thirty-nine articles. The wealth of Protestant doctrine is like that presented in Samuel Butler's Musical Banks in *Erewhon*. The cheques are like condoms – rubber, bounceable, sterile – and carry the number DUD 1132, signifying a false fall and a false resurrection. All this is pure dream-substance if not the dream-language Joyce has spent hundreds of pages teaching us. We can best interpret that disturbing near-clarity as an appropriate medium for the dreams of the morning, when daylight is contending with the kingdom of the dark. Here it is again, in the dialogue of the crosstalk comedians Muta and Juva:

MUTA: So that when we shall have acquired unification we shall pass on to diversity and when we shall have passed on to diversity we shall have acquired the instinct of combat and when we shall have acquired the instinct of combat we shall pass back to the spirit of appeasement?

JUVA: By the light of the bright reason which day sends to us from the high.

It is almost waking language but not quite.

As we should expect, the sleeping language is at its most difficult when the dream is at its deepest. The most complex part of the whole fabric is to be found in the scene where Earwicker is rent and consumed by his customers. The setting is a familiar locale, the pub itself, but the modulations of the language seem to take us to Leopardstown races, the Crimean War, the Scandinavia of the sagas, as well as to the Phoenix Park of HCE's alleged crime:

When old the wormd was a gadden and Anthea first unfoiled her limbs wanderloot was the way the wood wagged where opter and apter were samuraised twimbs. They had their mutthering ivies and their murdhering idies and their mouldhering iries in that muskat grove but there'll be bright plinnyflowers in Calomella's cool bowers when the magpyre's babble towers scorching and screeching from the ravenindove.

To attempt a close analysis of this, a typical passage, is to invite madness. But that the sound is meant to be more important than the sense becomes clear when we copy it out in song-form:

> When old the wormd was a gadden
> And Anthea first unfoiled her limbs
> Wanderloot was the way the wood wagged
> Where opter and apter were samuraised twimbs.
> They had their mutthering ivies
> And their murdhering idies
> And their mouldhering iries
> In that muskat grove.
> But there'll be bright plinnyflowers
> In Calomella's cool bowers
> When the magpyre's babble towers
> Scorching and screeching from the ravenindove.

Already it seems more approachable. Anthea is conventionalised into a stock song-nymph from the seventeenth century; her etymology tells us that the whole theme is floral. Relaxed, we allow her to settle into a version of Isobel, while the birdlike 'samuraised twimbs' become Shem and Shaun, her brothers. The primal garden has a worm or dragon in it. The ivy, like a crowd full of watching eyes, will see a murder on the Ides of March. The rainbow of peace, blooming as an iris, will lose its colours and decay. The musky grove is full of guns. HCE, who has defiled the garden with his crime, must be burnt, and then peace and fragrance will return to Eden. Those of us who are not satisfied until words yield a separable meaning may throw such an interpretation to the hungry dog of reason. Then, content with colour and rhythm, we can enjoy the passage as Joyce, presumably, wanted us to enjoy it.

Here is part of Earwicker's defence:

Missaunderstaid. Meggy Guggy's giggag. The code's proof! The rebald danger with they who would bare whiteness against me I

dismissem from the mind of good. He can tell such as story to the
Twelfth Maligns that my first was a nurssmaid and her fellower's a
willbe perambulatrix. There are twingty to twangty too thews and
leathermail coatschemes penparing to hostpost for it valinnteerily
with my valued fofavour to the post puzzles deparkment with larch
parchels' of presents for future branch offercings. The green approve
the raid! Shaum Baum's bode he is amustering in the groves while his
shool comes merging along! Want I put myself in their kirtlies I were
ayearn to leap with them and show me to bisextine.

There is a good deal of deliberate confusion here, though very
little guilty stuttering. Some of the wordplay becomes clear when
we speak it aloud – 'the green approve the /reːd/' – or sing it:
'Shaum Baum's bode he . . .' The two girls whom HCE saw in
the part were apparently wheeling a pram. There is a nice Freud-
ian touch in 'bare whiteness'. The twelve customers who are
always ready to pronounce verdicts are malignant. Earwicker's
sons – pen and post – are ambiguously involved in the trans-
mission of the truth, but it is clear that HCE is going to be
superseded, his body rent and distributed as gift parcels. Shaun,
as a tree, is preparing to rule the grove. Poor HCE would like to
join the twenty-eight girls who are Shaun's adorers. But it is
still, despite his self-exculpation, the leap-year girl – Isobel, his
own daughter – he is after. Yet, like music, this passage is finally
to be accepted as what it is, not what it is about. And, of course,
so is the whole book.

A good deal of *Finnegans Wake*, though it looks like prose, is
verse. When Hosty the rann-maker – who is probably Shaun in
disguise – leads the crowd against Earwicker, this is the song that
is sung:

Dour douchy was a sieguldson. He cooed that loud nor he was young.
He cud bad caw nor he was gray Like wather parted from the say.*

There are several stanzas. The twelve vindicative customers are,
before HCE's 'lyncheon party' begins, tucked up inside an 'Omar
Khayyam' *rubaiy*:

And thus within the tavern's secret booth The wisehight
ones who sip the tested sooth Bestir them as the Just has
bid to jab The punch of quaram on the mug of truth.

* 'Like water parted from the sea' – the refrain is from a song by Arne. The
  song, incidentally, was sung by John Keats when the ship on which he was
  travelling to Italy (to die in Rome) sprang a leak off the English coast.

Much earlier, Shaun reviles Shem in a parody of Thomas Campbell's poem about the Exile of Erin:

If you met on the binge a poor acheseyeld from Ailing, when the tune of his tremble shook shimmy on shin, while his countrary raged in the weak of his wailing, like a rugilant pugilant Lyon O'Lynn . . . if the fain shinner pegged you to shave his immartial, wee skillmustered shoul with his ooh, hoodoodoo! broking wind that to wiles, woemaid sin he was partial, we don't think, Jones, we'd care to this evening, would you?

(This, incidentally, is very much Joyce himself, 'ailing' with his 'acheseyeld') There are poems set as poems, like the end of the tale of the Ondt and the Gracehoper:

> *He larved and he larved on he merd such a nauses*
> *The Gracehoper feared he would mixplace his fauces.*
> *I forgive you, grondt Ondt, said the Gracehoper, weeping,*
> *For their sukes of the sakes you are safe in whose keeping.*
> *Teach Floh and Luse polkas, show Bienie where's sweet*
> *And be sure Vespatilla fines fat ones to heat . . .*

Or the admirable free verse of the Mamalujo quartet:

> *You won't need be lonesome, Lizzy my love, when your beau*
> *   gets his glut of cold meat and hot soldiering*
> *Nor wake in winter, window machree, but snore sung in my*
> *   old Balbriggan surtout.*
> *Wisha, won't you agree now to take me from the middle, say,*
> *   of next week on, for the balance of my days, for nothing*
> *   (what?) as your own nursetender?*
> *A power of highsteppers dies game right enough – but who,*
> *   acushla, 'll beg coppers for you?*

The song called 'The Ballad of Persse O'Reilly' is presented complete with music. The tune is twelve bars long – one bar for each of the twelve carpers – and seems to be of Neapolitan origin. It is apparently for alto voice, since it is written on a treble stave and goes down to G below middle C. Any male singer approaching it would demand that it be re-written an octave higher on the treble stave or transferred to the bass stave an octave lower. Like the version of the ballad of the Jew's daughter's killing of Hugh of Lincoln sung in *Ulysses* – which is too low for Stephen's tenor voice and is, indeed, written as for a baritone – there is something subtly wrong, or subtly symbolic, about it. Perhaps the fusion of Stephen and Bloom is figured in the deeper pitch, and the impending burial of HCE is suggested by most of the notes of the hymn of hate being thrust below the stave. Here it is as it might be performed on the viola d'amore, with singer in unison:

It was during some fresh water garden pumping Or, ac–

cording to the *Nursing Mirror* while admiring the monkeys That our

heavyweight heathen Humpharey made bold a maid to

woo Woo hoo, what'll she doo! The gen'ral

lost her maiden. . . . . loo!

This is not the melody as Joyce presents it in the book. After the first stanza the words fail to fit the tune. The above is one way in which an adjustment can be made for one of the easier of the later verses.

All this dream-poetry and song relates the *Wake* to the *Alice* books. The right to break without warning into metrical forms, sometimes of great strictness, is one of the gifts we assume is granted to the dreaming literary mind. But what haunts the ear most after a reading of the *Wake* is the rhythm of a particular sort

of prose structure. Much of the book suggests the gentle mockery
of the kind of sentence we associate with works of serious learning,
full of qualification, periodic, very long, though the *Wake*
content lurches in a seasick manner from the learned to the colloquial:

Now (to forebare for ever solittle of Iris Trees and Lili O'Rangans),
concerning the genesis of Harold or Humphrey Chimpden's occupa-
tional agnomen (we are back in the presurnames prodromarith period,
of course just when enos chalked halltraps) and discarding once for
all those theories from older sources which would link him back with
such pivotal ancestors as the Glues, the Gravys, the Northeasts, the
Ankers and the Earwickers of Sidlesham in the Hundred of Manhood
or proclaim him offsprout of vikings who had founded wapentake
and seddled hem in Herrick or Eric, the best authenticated version, the
Dumlat, read the Reading of Hofed-ben-Edar, has it that it was this
way. We are told how in the beginning it came to pass . . .

And so it goes on. The tone of most of the narrative – or pseudo-
historical – passages is both forbidding and seductive at the same
time. The taleteller or teacher seems thoroughly at ease with us
the audience, assuming a tradition in which attention is given
spontaneously, there are no watches to look at, interruptions are
allowed, drinks are served during the séance. We know how
Joyce piled on more and more allusions, admitted longer and
longer parentheses, on the ground of a fairly simple structure:
the drafts of the *Wake* show us most of the secrets. But the secrets
of building *Wake* sentences were never ones to be well kept. The
hero is an architect, and there is no mystery about raising even a
'waalworth of a skyerscape of most eyeful hoyth entowerly'.
We are all HCE, and we are at liberty to build for ourselves. The
technique is clear and, to fill the long winter evenings, it can be
exercised in ludic form. Thus:

Construct a sentence in Joycean oneiroglot, with at least five long
subordinate clauses and three or four parentheses. The subject shall
be the origin of the legend of Martin Luther's six toes on the left foot.
Present Luther as both a bird and a musical instrument.

To bigsing mitt (and there are some of sinminstral hexacordiality
who have cheeped Nine! Nine! to so supernumerapodical a valgar
halluxination of their Herro) it was harpbuzzing tags when, achording
to Fussboden and Sexfanger, the gamut and spinet of it was (A! O!
says Rholy with his Alfa Romega) that funf went into sox and Queen

Kway was half dousin to her sixther, so that our truetone orchestinian
luter (may his bother martins swallow rondines and roundels of
chelidons and their oves be eaved on the belfriars), deptargmined not
to be housesmartined by his frival sinxters (Ping! wint the strongs of
the eadg be guitarnberg), put hexes on his hocks and said sex is funf,
which is why he aspiered to a dietty of worms and married anon
(Moineau! Consparrocy!) after he had strummed his naughntytoo
frets on the door (fish can nosh tenders) and was eggscomeinacrated.

It is the raising of storey after storey, or the extension of the
message, which makes the *Wake* long. But there is also a rather
grim love of particularity, expressed in fantastically lengthy
catalogues. There are, for instance, the names that HCE is called
while he is in prison, some of which are as follows:

*Firstnighter, Informer, Old Fruit, Yellow Whigger, Wheatears, Goldy Geit,
Bogside Beauty, Yass We've Had His Badannas, York's Porker, Funnyface,
At Baggotty's Bend He Bumped, Grease with the Butter, Opendoor Ospices,
Cainandabler, Ireland's Eighth Wonderful Wonder, Beat My Price, Godsoilman,
Moonface the Murderer, Hoary Hairy Hoax, Midnight Sunburst, Remove that
Bible, Hebdromadary Publocation, Tummer the Lame the Tyrranous . . .*

And there are the three full pages giving the various names that
Anna Livia's 'untitled mamafesta' has been called in its long
history. The list begins with *The Angusta Angustissimost for Old
Seabeastius' Salvation* and ends with *First and Last Only True
Account all about the Honorary Mirsu Earwicker, L.S.D., and the
Snake (Nuggets!) by a Woman of the World who only can Tell Naked
Truths about a Dear Man and all his Conspirators how they all Tried
to Fall him Putting it all around Lucalizod about Privates Earwicker
and a Pair of Sloppy Sluts plainly showing all the Unmentionability
falsely Accusing about the Raincoats.* First and last, it is clear that her
aim is to defend the reputation of her dead lord. Once, some
readers think, would have been enough. When this same dead
lord is broken into fragments to provide 'a Christmas box for
aisch and iveryone of her childer', the number of these childer
is revealed as 111 – symbol of plenitude. The list of gifts and
names may be fantastic, but the total number plods on to the end,
clear and countable. Joyce's view is that generalisations are
unacceptable in dreams. Real life may admit algebra, but in our
sleep we arithmetise. The particularising lust may be seen interest-
ingly in the childhood scene where Shem, called there Glugg,

turns himself into James Joyce and goes in for 'scribenery with
the satiety of arthurs'. He proposes to write *Ulysses*, which has
already been mentioned in an earlier chapter as the 'Blue Book
of Eccles'. Now it is presented through parodic versions of the
Homeric titles of Bloom's Odyssey, from 'Lotus Eaters' on
(the Telemachia and Nostos are omitted): 'Ukalepe. Loathers'
Leave. Nemo in Patria. The Luncher Out. Skilly and Carubdish.
A Wondering Wreck. From the Mermaids' Tavern. Bullyfamous.
Naughtyscalves. Mother of Misery. Walpurgas Nacht.' This
technique suggests other games.

1. Punbaptise the names of the months from the viewpoint of a
   confirmed drunkard.
   Ginyouvery Pubyoumerry Parch Grapeswill Tray Juinp Droolie
   Sawdust Siptumbler Actsober Newwinebar Descendbeer.
2. If Charles Dickens could be dreamed of as a cook, what books
   might he be dreamed of as having frittern?
   Charred Limes. Grate Expectorations. The Cold Curried Sausagy
   Chop. Our Muttonual Fried. Halibut Twiced. Pickweak Peppers.
   Snack Elly's Knucklebone.

Not a very good cook.

The 'crossmess parzel' element in the *Wake* expresses itself
often in riddles. There is, for instance, a long riddling or quiz
session with the salutation 'Who do you no tonigh, lazy and
gentleman?' The lazy one is Shem, and Shaun is the gentleman,
a prize quizkid who 'rated one hundrick and thin per store-
hundred on this nightly quisquiquock of the twelve apostrophes,
set by Jockit Mic Ereweak'. Is 'Jockit' Shaun (John, Jack,
Jock) or Shem (Jacob, Jockib)? There are, as so often, two
answers. The first quiz question is thirteen pages long; it seeks
the identity of a 'maximost bridgesmaker' who stutters 'fore
he falls and goes mad entirely when he's waked; is Timb to the
pearly morn and Tomb to the mourning night', and so on. We
know the answer without being told, but we are told just the
same: 'Finn MacCool!' A question about the capitals of the four
Irish provinces has as answer: 'Delfas; Dorhqk; Nublid; Dalway'.
It is only the twelfth and last question that causes difficulty,
along with its answer. '*Sacer esto?*' asks the quizmaster, and the
reply comes: '*Semus sumus!*' Shaun is asking his brother both
'Are you blessed?' and 'Are you accursed?' Shem says: 'We

are Shem!' but also 'We are the same!' The spirit of Nolan Bruno is at work, shedding blessed or cursed ambiguity. In the scene devoted to children's games, where riddling is especially appropriate, Shem – called Glugg – is presented with a curious conundrum that is mimed by the girls of St Bride's. He is asked to guess what a particular colour is. Its elements are 'up tightly in the front . . . down again on the loose . . . drim and drumming on her back . . . and a pop from her whistle'. These turn out to be descriptive of some of the phonemes in the word *heliotrope*. Joyce, though no phonetician, is accurate enough. The /hiːlɪ/ is indeed high and well forward, the /ə/ loose or slack, the /tr/ first 'drimming' and then 'drumming on her back' as it moves to the back vowel, the /p/ a pop if not quite a whistling one. Shem cannot answer the riddle, and he at once wets his trousers. Asked another – 'Find the frenge for frocks and translace it into shocks of such as touch with show and show' – he again can find no answer, so he is told 'Get!'

Instinctively, in this section, Joyce has anticipated one of the findings of Claude Lévi-Strauss. If Shem is accepted by the month-girls he will be led to the act of love with the leapyear girl. As she is his own sister, he will be committing incest. Lévi-Strauss has shown the prevalence in primitive cultures of the relationship between riddling and incest. The best-known example in our own culture is provided by Oedipus, who had to be successful in answering the riddle of the Sphinx before he could go on to the killing of his father and the marrying of his own mother. Shem is saved from incest by his ineptitude in answering the riddles of the girls, who forthwith reject him. The wetting of his trousers draws our attention to the sexual significance of the riddles. In the *Wake*, semen and urine usually appear as the one fluid. As Bloom is saved from folly in Nighttown by his ejaculation on the beach, so Shem is saved from sin by his own incontinence, a symbol of his stupidity or innocence.

The chapter that follows the scene of the children's play presents Shem and Shaun at their schoolwork. It is crammed with riddles, most of which appear in the footnotes and the marginal glosses. The scope of the studies the boys must pursue is indicated thus:

Quick lunch by our left, wheel, to where. Long Livius Lane, mid Mezzofanti Mall, diagnosing Lavatery Square, up Tycho Brache

Crescent, shouldering Berkeley Alley, querfixing Gainsborough Carfax, under Guido d'Arezzo's Gadeway, by New Livius Lane till where we whiled while we whithered. Old Vico Roundpoint.

This itinerary covers the seven main branches of knowledge, beginning with Livy the historian and ending with him. Vico is present to remind the students of the circular nature of history. Joyce cannot resist emphasising Guido d'Arezzo's particular contribution to the art of music. In 'Gadeway' we are reminded, punningly, of his doctrine of tuning: G A D E are still, though not in that order, the four open strings of the violin. The footnotes do not always refer directly to the items numbered in the text: they often form a riddling pattern of their own. Those on the first page, for instance, are as follows:

1 Rawmeash, quoshe with her girlic teangue. If old Herod with the Cormwell's eczema was to go for me like he does Snuffler whatever about his blue canaries I'd do nine months for his beaver beard.

2 Mater Mercy Mercerycordial of the Dripping Nipples, milk's a queer arrangement.

3 Real life behind the floodlights as shown by the best exponents of a royal divorce.

This seems to be Isobel commenting on the father-God theme which the two brothers must study first. That element '-meash' evidently echoes the 'mishe mishe' of the very first page of the book, turning her into a St Bridget, symbol of Irish womanhood, and, by extension, symbol of all women. The bearded God, in the form of a bird, impregnates her. But the third footnote, referring to Earwicker's favourite play – *A Royal Divorce* (a once very popular *drame* about Napoleon and Josephine) – secularises the theme. God, like Father Christmas, is only one's own father. One suspects (and the *Ricorso* proves one right) that he is not getting on very well with one's mother.

Some of the footnote riddles are in plain English, but they are as mad as the richest of Joyce's jabberwocky. It is the relevance, not the sense, that is elusive. 'All the world loves a big gleaming jelly' is probably true, or at least an advertisement might assume it to be true, but it means little, or seems to, in terms of the *Wake* – unless, of course, the jelly is Shaun, swollen specious innutritious demagogue. The word 'brandnewburgher' in the text is defined in the footnotes as 'A viking vernacular expression still

used in the Summerhill district for a jerryhatted man of forty who
puts two fingers into his boiling soupplate and licks them in
turn to find out if there is enough mushroom catsup in the
mutton broth'. At odd moments in the last thirty years I have
had a febrile conviction that I understood Joyce's deep meaning –
usually in illness or the middle of the night. In waking health I
remain ignorant. At last, though, I understand 'Gee each owe
tea eye smells fish'. I recognised on first reading the allusion to
Bernard Shaw's views on English orthography – *fish* can logi-
cally be spelt with the *gh* in *laugh*, the *o* in *women* and the *ti* in
nation – but it has taken me a long time to see that, in religious
symbology, a fish may well have a goaty or ghoti smell. Christ,
the fish, replaces the *tragos* of the Old Law; he also has the odour
of a scapegoat.

Verse, catalogues, riddles, 'hierarchitectitiptitoploftical' sentences help to weave the thick texture of *Finnegans Wake*. The larger
structural problem is less weighty than in *Ulysses*. The task of
carrying the narrative is given to a universal mind which resem-
bles Joyce's but is probably really Finnegan's, capable of a wide
range of deformed colloquial, twisted learning and parody; it is
also given to characters within the dream – the washerwomen
who, turning respectively to a tree and a stone, can be identified
with Shem (Stem) and (Stone) Shaun; Earwicker himself; Anna
Livia, especially in the closing monologue; even the donkey
(who may be Christ) that follows the four old men. There are
fables, a quiz, a textbook, but there is no dramatic edifice corresponding to the 'Circe' episode of *Ulysses*. The crosstalk characters, Jute and Mutt, who end up as Muta and Juva, break the
narrative sequences with patches of raw dialogue, but their turns
are brief. At the beginning of Book II Joyce seems to promise a
dramatic entertainment. He gives us a cast-list for a play he calls
The Mime of Mick, Nick and the Maggies but becomes more
interested in having us read the programme than in mounting a
drama:

With futurist onehorse balletbattle pictures and the Pageant of Past
History worked up with animal variations amid everglaning man-
grovemazes and beorbtracktors by Messrs Thud and Blunder. Shadows
by the film folk, masses by the good people. Promptings by Elanio
Vitale. Longshots, upcloses, outblacks and stagetolets by Hexen-
schuss, Coachmaher, Incubone and Rocknarrag. Creations tastefully

designed by Madame Berthe Delamode. Dances arranged by Harley Quinn and Coollimbeina.

In fact, more than in *Ulysses*, Joyce is concerned with bookness, the whatness of Allbook. We must never be allowed to forget that we are reading. Sounds and scenes and characters may start up from the page, but they are not permitted to move off it. Mick, Nick and the Maggies perform, but not in light similar to the phantasmagoric spots and floods of Nighttown: there has to be a thick fog of language whose elements are to be seen as well as heard. A work which seems to invoke the preliterate past of legend and myth only does so etymologically, for a legend is something to be read and a myth is a tale and a tale is something carved with a knife. The thick chords of language have to be cut, and usually only the eye can cut them.

CHAPTER II

Language of the People

𝕊𝕊𝕊𝕊𝕊𝕊

DESPITE an ambition for artistic self-effacement more fanatical even than Flaubert's, the personality of James Joyce shines through all his work, especially as expressed in his tastes and allegiances. When he went into exile, he took with him an uneffaceable image of the Dublin he had known as a boy and knew as a young man, but he also took with him the lineaments of the adolescent mind that formed that image. To a great extent he was always Stephen Dedalus, capable of *fin de siècle* languor, the posturings of the misunderstood aesthete, the pale poetry of immaturity. Nora Joyce was quick to rebuke these attitudes with common sense and strong tea. Nevertheless, Joyce's nostalgia for his youth was more than self-indulgence: that youth represented a complex sensibility that had been able to nourish a long tradition of art but was now in the process of rapid liquidation. The middle ages knew the poor scholar who was better acquainted with low taverns, cutpurses, prostitutes, argot, the intricate labyrinths of the slums, than with money for square meals, respectability, the elevations of life proper to learning. Perhaps for the last time in literary history, the novels of Joyce celebrate the confluence of curious erudition and the language of the streets. The university students of today do not, as Dr Johnson did, walk around with their toes sticking out of their boots, unless this happens to be an aspect of student *couture*, and they do not hug tattered books joyfully picked up on street-stalls. Enforced urban poverty and higher education no longer go together. This is good, but it means no more Stephen Dedaluses.

The Catholic Church had a good deal to do with reconciling, in Joyce's nascent creative imagination, the opposed claims of academic learning and the depraved life of a poor city. Latin was the language of Virgil and Horace, poets read by the few, but also the language of the mass, heard and partially understood by the many. The emancipated Stephen Dedalus makes an aesthetic philosophy out of St Thomas Aquinas; to mention that holy doctor in a Dublin pub would not necessarily provoke the low-brow scorn it would meet in an English roadhouse. Entering the brothel district with Lynch, Stephen intones the introit for paschal time: '*Vidi aquam egredientem de templo a latere dextro.*' It is not all that bizarre a thing to do in a Catholic slum, though the bawd who hears him associates the Latin with Trinity College, not UCD, and medical students: 'Fallopian tube. All prick and no pence.' The only sizeable piece of secular Latin we hear in *Ulysses* is this of Cicero's:

Talis ac tanta depravatio hujus seculi, O quirites, ut matres familiarum nostrae lascivas cujuslibet semiviri libici titillationes testibus ponderosis atque excelsis erectionibus centurionum Romanorum magnopere anteponunt.

This is perhaps the one fragment of ancient literature which joins together the low and the high. I have heard it recited, though in translation, in more than one army mess, usually by a senior quartermaster. In its original form it fits well into the bibulous nocturne of a town that accepts Latin even if only on Sundays and holy days of obligation.

The name of Aristotle occurs frequently in *Ulysses*, and it may be regarded as another link between the town and the gown. Aristotle to Stephen and his intellectual equals means the Stagyrite; to Bloom, and to most others on his educational level, it means the monk who wrote a treatise on obstetrics. Cockney rhyming slang celebrates Aristotle – he stands for *bottle*; *bottle and glass* stands for *arse*, and so does the abbreviation *Aris* – and it is probably the author of the book seen in rubber-shop windows who is meant, not the master of them that know. The 'Oxen of the Sun' chapter – from which I have taken the Cicero (or alleged Cicero) – quietly glorifies the two Aristotles in one in the Gibbon pastiche: 'all the cases of human nativity which Aristotle has classified in his masterpiece with chromolithographic illustrations.' Aristotle rings one bell for Stephen, another for Bloom (for whom the 'chromolithographic illustrations' – which he has noticed earlier that day on a bookstall – are specifically meant).

The music of the Catholic services is known to both Stephen and Bloom, and it is an obvious enharmonic chord for modulating from one world to the other, but Bloom knows it through his

wife's participation in works like the *Stabat Mater*, while Stephen
and the ignorant Catholic poor know it as a common part of
their lives. At a level above pub singing and barrel organs,
Stephen's Italian is not as remote from popular music as it would
be in today's Dublin. In the 'Sirens' scene, the titles of arias are
always given in Italian, even though the words of the arias are
only known in translation. Mr Dedalus is asked to sing *M'appari*
and at once breaks into 'When first I saw that form endearing'.
Stephen's culture has, despite its depth, width and rarifaction,
superficial areas in common with that of uneducated Dubliners.
For Stephen, read Joyce. Apart from book-learning, Joyce's
upbringing lacked many things that are now taken for granted
in capital cities and, in consequence, not much valued. He
shared with all his fellow-citizens the lack of opportunity of
hearing much music outside the repertoire, secular and sacred,
of the Carl Rosa Opera Company. There were no symphony
concerts or *lieder* recitals, and in Joyce's works there are no
references to purely orchestral music or to vocal music in which
the accompaniment is as important as the melodic line. Though
pictorial art is president of 'Nausicaa', there is no real tribute
to it except in the static composition of the scene and the occasional use of the word *tableau*. Joyce's lack of knowledge of
painting and sculpture is not altogether a consequence of his
not being able to rely much on his eyes: after all, Aldous Huxley
went near-blind after a lifetime of ocular trouble and is still the
best-informed of all novelists on the history and aesthetics of
painting. There were just no pictures to see in Dublin; Joyce
had no chance of becoming trained in the visual arts.

The arts which were important to Joyce – music and literature –
were, at one level or another, important to all Dubliners. If
little poetry was read by the pub-crawlers, at least they knew
some poetry by heart because they knew some songs by heart –
the lyrics of Thomas Moore, for instance. And, preceding all
concern with literature, there was a powerful instinct for the
phatic or persuasive use of language. Music and talk would first
be met, plentifully if not variously, in the family circle. It is
possible to say of *Finnegans Wake* that it glorifies a sort of culture
of deprivation, but this is another way of saying that it exalts
the culture of the family. The book resolves itself into a compendium of what children play in the street, the private language

they use round the fire, the songs they sing at the piano in the Sunday parlour. When Joyce, like Stephen, left his father's house, it was only to become a father himself and to cherish – as no other author has – the virtues of domesticity (a word which contains both *demos* and *city*).

The reader of *Finnegans Wake* knows that, to Joyce, history could be regarded as an emanation of family: the twins fight, and they are Cain and Abel but also Napoleon and Wellington; the father and mother dream of a royal divorce; Cleopatra and Kitty O'Shea are embodied in the daughter who flaunts her new nubility. But the language, as opposed to the enactments, is never much in disguise. The book is full of the language of family:

You'll catch it, don't fret, Mrs Tummy Lupton! Come indoor, Scoffy-nosey, and shed your swank!

The nurse'll give it you, stickypots! And you wait, my lasso, fecking the twine.

You're well held now, Missy Cheekspeer, and your panto's off!
Ah, crabeyes, I have you, showing off to the world with that gape in your stocking!

The pram-language of Cissy Caffrey in 'Nausicaa' provides certain basic rhythms for both books: 'What's your name? Butter and cream?' 'O my! Puddeny pie! He has his bib destroyed' and 'Here's the lord mayor, here's his gingerbread carriage and here he walks in, chinchopper, chinchopper, chin'. And one childish trope is common to both; it evidently fascinated Joyce, being perhaps one of the 'epiphanies', or revelations of reality, he was always seeking. The 'education' chapter of the *Wake* has, as marginal gloss: 'MAWMAW, LUK, YOUR BEEFTAY'S FIZZIN OVER!' These are words used by Master Patrick Aloysius Dignam in the 'Circe' section of *Ulysses*. Very few of the major characters of both books wholly forget the sounds and emphases of childhood speech – meaning, of course, that Joyce does not forget them. In *Stephen Hero*, the children with whom Stephen plays call out a jingle based on a Christian name, like this on Stephen's own: 'Stephen, the Reeven, the Rix Dix Deeven'. Stephen notices that his doomed sister Isobel never hears her name so jangled, and attributes this to her own with-drawnness, her lack of vitality, her doomedness. Bloom is not doomed; 'Circe' presents him, in one stage-direction, as 'Poldy, the rix dix doldy'.

The *Wake* is capable of folding us all into a childhood world – convincingly, tenderly, without A. A. Milne whimsy. The prayer that is spoken for Shem, Shaun and Isobel (nothing of that doomed sister in her, despite the associations that must have clung to the name when Joyce chose it) is, despite its ingenuity, touching:

O Loud, hear the wee beseech of thees of each of these thy unlitten ones! Grant sleep in hour's time, O Loud!

That they take no chill. That they do ming no merder. That they shall not gomeet madhowiatrees.

Loud, heap miseries upon us yet entwine our arts with laughters low!

Ha he hi ho hu.

Mummum.

The preoccupation with urine and faeces, remarked on unfavourably by many *Wake* commentators, is fitting in the familial context of the whole work. 'That they do ming no merder' (Latin *mingere*, French *merde*) can be a heartfelt prayer for a family too poor for ample changes of bed-linen. This bedtime orison embraces all of us, even the animals in the Phoenix Park zoo. With Joyce there is no shame in being brought down to the child's level. It is hard to imagine such unabashed indulgence in babytalk in Virginia Woolf or E. M. Forster.

Children's rhymes are popular with Joyce, as also the less innocent verses of adolescence. 'Circe' gives us a prospectus from infantility to delinquency. The Babes and Sucklings cry to Bloom:

> Clap clap hands till Poldy comes home,
> Cakes in his pocket for Leo alone.

Zoe the prostitute tells Bloom:

> Give a thing and take it back
> God'll ask you where is that
> You'll say you don't know
> God'll send you down below.

The Artane orphans sing to him:

> You hig, you hog, you dirty dog!
> You think the ladies love you!

And, obscenely, the Prison Gate girls:

> If you see kay
> Tell him he may
> See you in tea
> Tell him from me.

At Bloom's trial, a voice from the gallery calls:

> Moses, Moses, king of the jews,
> Wiped his arse in the Daily News.

Schoolgirls, I seem to remember, had a euphemistic version of this:

> Nebuchadnezzar the king of the Jews
> Bought his wife a pair of shoes.

Joyce's taste in song is considered vulgar. The operatic arias in *Ulysses*, apart from Molly Bloom's *La ci darem*, which has depressing associations of adultery, are mostly from works of the second or third rank – *The Bohemian Girl*, *Martha*, *The Lily of Killarney*. Most of the other songs are from pantomime or music-hall. Stephen remembers his mother laughing at 'old Royce in the pantomime of Turko the terrible'. He sang:

> I am the boy
> That can enjoy
> Invisibility.

Mulligan sings a song dating from Edward VII's coronation, but he does not get it quite right:

> O, won't we have a merry time
> Drinking whisky, beer and wine,
> On Coronation,
> Coronation day?

The words should be:

> We'll be merry,
> Drinking whisky, beer and sherry,
> All be merry
> On Coronation Day.

Bloom, having expressed his love for his daughter in the following popular family rhyme:

> O, Milly Bloom, you are my darling,
> You are my looking glass from night to morning,
> I'd rather have you without a farthing
> Than Katey Keogh with her ass and garden,

is haunted all day by Boylan's song about the seaside girls:

> All dimpled cheeks and curls,
> Your head it simply swirls.

He hears 'flat Dublin voices . . . in his head' singing:

> O, Mary lost the pin of her drawers.
> She didn't know what to do
> To keep it up
> To keep it up.

In 'Circe' it is Leopold who is alleged to have lost it. Anything with drawers in it went straight to Joyce's heart: he had a miniature pair as a top pocket handkerchief. In *A Portrait* we hear:

> Lottie Collins lost her drawers.
> Won't you kindly lend her yours?

(It is in *A Portrait* that Cranly's words – '*Mulier cantat*' – glorify the sound of a scullerymaid singing 'Sweet Rosie O'Grady' and bring together three worlds.) And, finally, if illicit love can be cosily blanketed by 'Love's Old Sweet Song', the overture to the destruction of time and space can be 'My Girl's a Yorkshire Girl'. Stephen, hitting the brothel chandelier with his ashplant, cries '*Nothung!*', but that is as near to a Wagnerian consummation as we get. Joyce provides his own heavy music in the words.

In *Finnegans Wake* popular songs are an essential part of the texture. Out of hundreds, a few examples will suffice:

They laid him brawdawn alanglast bed. With a bockalips of finisky fore his feet. And a barrowload of guenesis hoer his head. Tee the tootal of the fluid hang the twoddle of the fuddled, O!

This is for Finnegan's funeral or funferall – a combination of the New York Irish ballad of Tim Finnegan the bricklayer and 'Phil the Fluter's Ball'.

Hay, hay, hay! Hoq, hoq, hoq! Faun and Flora on the lea love that little old joq.

That is 'Little Brown Jug'. Here is a fusion of 'Little Dolly Daydream' and a song that names itself:

But there's a little lady waiting and her name is A.L.P. And you'll agree. She must be she. For her holden heirheaps hanging down her back,

And this ends as 'Auld Lang Syne':

The quad gospellers may own the targum but any of the Zingari shoolerim may pick a peck of kindlings yet from the sack of auld hensyne.

The 'auld hen' is Belinda, who scratches up ALP's letter from a mound of rubbish and merits the Newmanian 'Lead kindly fowl'. The quiz on the characters of the *Wake* introduces the barman Sackerson or Saunderson with Stephen Foster's 'Poor old Jo(e)' and Kate the cleaning-woman with the words 'Summon in the housesweep Dina', which refers back to the blackface song in *Ulysses*:

> There's someone in the house with Dinah,
> There's someone in the house, I know.
> There's someone in the house with Dinah,
> Playing on the old banjo.

A brief string of song reminiscences appears when Shem asks the question 'When is a man not a man?' (answer: 'When he is a Sham'):

One said when the heavens are quakers, a second said when Bohemeand lips, a third said when he, no, when hold hard a jiffy, when he is a gnawstick and detarmined to . . . still another said when the wine's at witsends, and still another when lovely wooman stoops to conk him, one of the littliest said me, me, Sem, when pappa papered the harbour . . . another when yes, he hath no mananas . . .

'When Bohemeand lips' refers both to *The Bohemian Girl* (so well-known in Joyce's Dublin that the *Wake* at one point refers to it merely as *The Bo' Girl*) and one of the songs in it: 'When other lips'. 'When pappa papered the harbour' has both HCE as an invading Northman and the Victorian 'When Father Papered the Parlour'. 'Yes, he hath no mananas' (meaning either that he is not given to procrastination or has no tomorrow, or both) refers to 'Yes, We Have no Bananas', popular the year *Ulysses* was published. Here is 'Ten men went to mow':

When men want to write a letters. Ten men, ton men, pen men, pun men, wont to rise a ladder. And den men, dun men, fen men, fun men, hen men, hun men, wend to raze a leader.

Taff's 'The rib, the rib, the quean of oldbyrdes' refers back, through 'leave it to Hosty for he's the mann to rhyme the rann, the rann, the rann, the king of all ranns', to *Ulysses*, *The Golden Bough* and an obscure ancient sacrificial killing:

> The wren, the bold wren, the king of all birds,
> Saint Stephen's his day, was caught in the furze.

Here, finally, is the spiritual 'I got shoes':

He goat a berth. And she cot a manege. And wohl's gorse mundom ganna wedst.

It seems that Joyce needs the well-known, even the banal, to hold down his verbal flights to a real remembered Dublin. If it is not song that is used, it is jingle – childish or commercial, always strongly alliterative:

That's enough, genral, of finicking about Finnegan and fiddling with his faddles.
Ghinees hies good for you.
So, nat by night by naught by naket, in those good old lousy days gone by . . .
My granvilled brandold Dublin lindub, the free, the froh, the frothy freshener.
niece by nice by neat by natty . . .

Or else it echoes a proverb or similar well-worn popular saying:

So that meal's dead off for summan, schlook, schlice and goodrid-hirring.
For a nod to the nabir is better than wink to the wabsanti.
It's an allavalonche that blows nopussy food.

But mostly it is a flow of demotic speech in which fragments of learning or newspaper reports or shopsigns have lodged. This speech is often working-class, not much different from the speech of the old peasantry:

I've an eye on queer Behan and old Kate and the butter, trust me. She'll do no jugglywuggly with her war souvenir postcards to help to build me murial, tippers. I'll trip your traps! Assure a sure there! And we put on your clock again, sir, for you. Did or didn't we, share-stutterers? So you won't be up a stump entirely. Nor shed your remnants. The sternwheel's crawling strong. I seen your missus in the hall. Like the queenoveire. Arrah, it's herself that's fine, too, don't be talking!

By the smell of her kelp they made the pigeonhouse. Like fun they did! But where was Himself, the timoneer? That marchantman he suivied their scutties right over the wash, his cameleer's burnous breezing up on him, till with his runagate bowmpriss he rode and borst her bar.

Sucho fuffing a fifeing 'twould cut you in two! She'd bate the hen that crowed on the turrace of Babbel. What harm if she knew how to cockle her mouth! And not a mag out of Hum no more than out of the mangle weight. Is that a faith? That's the fact.

Encouraged by his need to deform the shape of words for punning purposes, Joyce is more willing than in *Ulysses* to indicate dialectal pronunciation. Indeed, it is paronomastically useful, in that last example, that *him* in Dublin speech should have a central vowel, for he is enabled to write it as 'Hum' and thus show that *him* was Humphrey.

There is a vulgar kind of lower middle class speech that Joyce is good at recording, and it is, in general, the monopoly of Shaun. It is the sleazy language of small salesmen and it is full of leering suggestiveness, weak blasphemy, and familiarity with cheap teashops. It comes out at its best, or worst, in Shaun's address to the month-girls:

Never miss your lostsomewhere mass for the couple in Myles you butrose to brideworship. Never hate mere pork which is bad for your knife of a good friday. Never let a hog of the howth trample underfoot your linen of Killiney. Never play lady's game for the Lord's stake. Never lose your heart away till you win his diamond back. Make a strong point of never kicking up your rumpus over the scroll ends of sofas in the Dar Bey Coll Cafeteria by tootling risky *apropos* songs at commercial travellers' smokers for their Columbian nights entertainments the like of *White limbs they never stop teasing* or *Minxy was a Manxmaid when Murry wor a Man* . . . First thou shalt not smile. Twice thou shalt not love. Lust, thou shalt not commix idolatry. Hip confiners help compunction. Never park your brief stays in the men's convenience . . . O foolish coupled! Ah, dice's error! Never dip in the ern while you've browsers on your suite. Never slip the silver key through your gate of golden age. Collide with man, collude with money.

And so on, for several pages. The last piece of advice in this excerpt is, I believe, already passing into the language. 'O foolish coupled' is the more vulgar for being a deformation of '*O felix culpa*' (acceptable enough as 'O Phoenix culprit'). A pleasant enough parlour song – 'White wings, they never grow weary' – is made unpleasantly greasy. The 'mere pork' near the beginning relates to Jonathan Swift, who is later in the book turned into the bird that cries 'more pork' – the reference being to the Moor Park where Swift was, as it were, caged by Sir William Temple. This idiolect can debase anything.

Joyce knew dialects that Virginia Woolf was debarred, by her upbringing more than her sex, from even wishing to get to know. Both Bloom and Stephen are fascinated by the life of the suburbs. Bloom imagines a brief scene which may be taken as an epiphany:

Hotblooded young student fooling round her fat arms ironing.
  – Are those yours, Mary?
  – I don't wear such things ... Stop or I'll tell the missus on you. Out half the night.
  – There are great times coming, Mary. Wait till you see.
  – Ah, get along with your great times coming.

But Stephen knows the speech of even the lowest prostitutes. Two words – 'Faster, darlint' – are enough to evoke 'Fumbally's lane that night: the tanyard smells'. The higher prostitutes – Florry, Zoe and Kitty – are capable of locutions like 'Ask my ballocks that I haven't got', but they disclose their lower middle class background in tropes like 'Forfeits, a fine thing and a superfine thing' (Zoe) and 'The bird that can sing and won't sing' (Florry of Stephen) and 'God help your head, he knows more than you have forgotten' (Zoe of Stephen to Lynch) and 'O, excuse!' (Kitty, having hiccupped). There is a fine smell of lowness in the account, in 'Cyclops', of Bob Doran in the prostitutes' den:

And the two shawls killed with the laughing, picking his pockets the bloody fool and he spilling the porter all over the bed and the two shawls screeching laughing at one another. *How is your testament? Have you got an old testament?*

It was Joyce's knowledge of the lower reaches of Dublin life, and his determination – following the naturalistic side of his symbolist naturalism – that its language should appear in a novel, along with certain basic aspects of middle-class life that had never previously been disclosed in fiction, that earned him certain ladylike rebukes from the British literary establishment, which did not like his cleverness or erudition either. In the first chapter of *Ulysses*, 'snotgreen' as an epithet for both Stephen's handkerchief and the waters of Dublin Bay caused some murmurs in the nineteen-twenties, and the naming of one character as Pisser Burke and another as Biddy the Clap and yet another as Cunty Kate contributed to the interest of the censors in Joyce's masterpiece. But there are more spectacular uses of obscene language, not now very remarkable, which attest a sharp ear and, what is – surprisingly – rarer, an understanding of the ways in which quadriliterals (as we may pedantically or Joyceanly call them) may properly be used. For D. H. Lawrence's *Lady Chatterley's Lover* shows that its author had been well shielded from the ways in which *cunt* and *fuck* are regularly employed, in their sexual significations, by the lower orders. Henry Miller uses these terms, and others, too freely – which devalues them – and feels, in his freedom, obliged to use them in contexts where they do not precisely fit. Molly Bloom, towards the end of her monologue, uses accurate language:

Ill let him know if thats what he wanted that his wife is fucked yes and damn well fucked too up to my neck nearly not by him 5 or 6 times handrunning

Fuck still carries a whiff of its origin. It is cognate with the German *ficken*, meaning 'to strike', and it has overtones of violence. It is not a tender word, and it cannot properly be used as Mr Kenneth Tynan once used it on BBC television (thus making history), in the context of a discussion of married love. A man does *not* fuck his wife: he makes love to her. Molly does not blame Bloom for a failure in fucking; indeed, she can find no ready term to describe the marital act. But she is right to associate the term with the bull-like Boylan. Bloom himself scarcely uses any of the basic sexual words, but there is one point in an early interior monologue where he produces one aptly, poetically, triumphantly:

The oldest people. Wandered far away over all the earth, captivity to captivity, multiplying, dying, being born everywhere. It lay there now. Now it could bear no more. Dead: an old woman's: the grey sunken cunt of the world.

He is thinking of the Levant that is his true Ithaca, No. 7 Eccles Street being the Calypso's cave where he is held in exile. The word *cunt*, with its plosives and nasal and short vowel, is no very apt word for a living vulva, but the quality of hardness and dryness it seems to carry is highly appropriate for Bloom's vision of a barren world. The term does not appear again, except in Kate's nickname and a single fantastic compound, and it is *quim* that Lenehan uses in the 'Circe' episode when asking Boylan about his latest conquests.

There are comparatively few examples of sexual terms used expletively in *Ulysses*, though Dubliners have not been noticeably more reluctant than Londoners to garnish their speech with four-letter snarls. It is rarely that the unnamed narrator of 'Cyclops' uses anything stronger than *bloody*, and all Mr Dedalus's bad language is made up of fecal references. As if foul words were a monopoly of the British lower classes, Joyce reserves his one and only obscene cadenza for Private Carr:

I'll do him in, so help me fucking Christ! I'll wring the bastard fucker's bleeding blasted fucking windpipe! [etc.]

Here we must imagine that the resources of reasonable or imaginative language have ceased to be available. Mindless violence requires the speech of the violently mindless.

Blasphemy appeals far more to Joyce than does obscenity. It is conceivably more shocking for a Catholic to indulge in this (a celebration of corporal punishment in the British Navy) than to burst out with four-letter words:

They believe in rod, the scourger almighty, creator of hell upon earth and in Jacky Tar, the son of a gun, who was conceived of unholy boast, born of the fighting navy, suffered under rump and dozen, was scarified, flayed and curried, yelled like bloody hell, the third day he rose again from the bed, steered into haven, sitteth on his beamend till further orders whence he shall come to drudge for a living and be paid.

Blasphemy, of a gentle and poetic kind, totally replaces obscenity in the *Wake*:

In the name of Annah the Allmaziful, the Everliving, the Bringer of Plurabilities, haloed be her eve, her singtime sung, her rill be run, unhemmed as it is uneven!

Sex itself, in that book, is soft-pedalled. There are no violent lust-scenes though there are plenty of exhibited drawers. The scatological symbolises the erotic, but even scatology is expressed periphrastically or euphemistically. *Incest* becomes *insect*, and pretty fables about Jabberwocklike creatures are raised on that creative metathesis. All the nastiness of the world is diluted into the nastiness of children who know no better.

Joyce's exploitation of the rhythms of popular speech achieves a great triumph in the final monologue of Ann Porter or Anna Livia Plurabelle, which is a far more masterly achievement – and far more moving – than the corresponding feminine ending of *Ulysses*. ALP appears as an ageing woman, as a child, as a river, as all rivers, and all at once. Facetious puns, scholarly loanwords, infantile memories, folk poetry are gathered into the stream as the wife turns from her husband and back to her 'cold mad feary father', the sea:

And can it be it's nnow fforvell? Illas! I wisht I had better glances to peer to you through this baylight's growing. But you're changing, acoolsha, you're changing from me, I can feel. Or is it me is? I'm getting mixed. Brightening up and tightening down. Yes, you're changing, sonhusband, and you're turning, I can feel you, for a daughterwife from the hills again.

In so all-inclusive an idiolect, the voice of the author himself can flash by for an instant, joining its plaint with that of his heroine:

A hundred cares, a tithe of troubles and is there one who understands me? Once in a thousand of years of the nights?

According to Richard Ellmann, there is an echo here of Joyce in his Trieste days, taking his son Giorgio to a toy fair to make up for his inability (they were very poor) to buy him a present:

So soft this morning, ours. Yes. Carry me along, taddy, like you done through the toy fair! If I seen him bearing down on me now under whitespread wings like he'd come from Arkangels, I sink I'd die down over his feet, humbly dumbly, only to washup. Yes tid., There's where. First. We pass through grass behush the bush to. Whish! A

gull. Gulls. Far galls, Coming, far! End here. Us then. Finn, again!
Bussoftlhee, mememormee! Till thousendsthee. Lps. The keys to.
Given! A way a lone a last a loved a long the

But the whole passage, besides being very moving, is a remarkable
summary of the resources of Joyce's essentially intimate language.
'Arkangels' has an astonishing resonance, and it can be juxtaposed without absurdity (or the traditional notion of absurdity)
with an image that, for a moment, turns the river back and thins
it to dishwater gurgling down the drain. 'Humbly dumbly'
sums it all up. The great egg who is also the mythical builder of
cities can modulate, with no strain, to mute servitude in so flex-
ible a language. There is no conflict between worshipping and
washing up. In 'Bussoftlhee, mememormee!' Joyce leaves
everything to sound, and there are few things in literature more
poignant than that dying moan – 'Remember me' with death
and marble and yet also a fluid watery murmur in the middle of
it. The keys unlock the door so that the woman of the house may
leave before anyone is up. But they also open up the gates of the
sea. The river flows away and then, on the first page of the book,
which we must once more engage, is seen in a kind of long shot,
the feminine principle 'commodiusly' married to the masculine,
incarnated in cities:

riverrun, past Eve and Adam's, from swerve of shore to bend of bay
brings us by a commodius vicus of recirculation to Howth Castle and
Environs.

It is these moments of poetic magic that reconcile the struggling
reader to the difficulties of *Finnegans Wake*, just as the humanity
and humour of *Ulysses* make him tolerant of experiments that
go on too long, or of linguistic displays that seem to subsist in
an unfruitful parallel to the narrative line. But fear of Joyce, and
distrust of his approach to language, remain commoner than the
kind of love accorded to such of his equals as Dickens, Balzac
or Tolstoy. He has to be viewed less from an avant-garde angle
than from one so traditional that, like Evelyn Waugh's conservat-
ism, it looks more radical than anarchism. Joyce is close to
Rabelais and Sterne, and a 'totality' of language which resolves
into the homely relates him to Shakespeare. I am speaking, of
course, mainly of *Ulysses*, which is more and more being accepted
as the product of a tradition older than naturalism and frequently

attacked now, not because it is unintelligible, but because it has become intelligible enough to disclose its faults. *Finnegans Wake*, despite the libraries of exegesis that have been erected, remains literally a closed book to the majority of serious readers of literature. Whether it is a success or a failure seems to me to be beside the point. It had to be written by somebody, and Joyce was available to write it. The world of sleep is a legitimate subject-matter for the novelist, but perhaps no verbal technique for expressing it could ever be wholly satisfactory. To use ordinary language would be to falsify, tacitly to interpret, not to present an objective image of the quality of the dreaming experience. Extraordinary language of any kind always causes murmurs, but the honest artist, committed to using it, must brave them. The commonest complaint heard about the language of *Finnegans Wake* is that it is *too* extraordinary, that Joyce should have been content with the mild and whimsical distortions of words that were so charming in his early drafts. This really means that he should have been content with what the native Latin-Teutonic stock could provide and not go searching through the vocabularies of foreign languages.

To anyone who does not know many, or any, foreign languages, such a view must seem just. The trouble is that when a writer goes, like Joyce, into exile, the term 'foreign' ceases to mean what it means to the stay-at-home. French, German and Italian were, according to his place of exile, tongues that were the daily medium of communication: Italian was, even when they were living in Paris, the first language of the Joyce family.* No writer who is aware of words can, in such circumstances, resist the fertilisation of his native tongue by ones that are not native. The multilingual life of Rudyard Kipling's work is full of Urdu, and nobody complains, though – lacking the environment in which an Indian tongue can alone yield its full meaning – not everybody can wholly understand. I myself was, for nearly six years, in such close touch with the Malay language that it affected my English and still affects my thinking. When I wrote a novel called *A Clockwork Orange*, no European reader saw that the Malay word for 'man' – *orang* – was contained in the title (Malay students of English invariably write 'orang squash' and no amount of correc-

* The prosodic pattern of the Twelve in the *Wake* may owe something to the clusters of like word-endings which characterise bureaucratic Italian.

tion will kill the habit). It is this sense of division between an author's own linguistic knowledge and that of his audience that will force him to restrict his use of loanwords or not to rely too much on the power of exotic connotation. Joyce would not, in *Finnegans Wake*, accept such a restriction: rather the opposite. He deliberately learned new languages to enrich the dream-texture of his book, convinced – perhaps wrongly – that this would emphasise the universality of his subject. Probably the essential motive derived from the limited punning possibilities available to English alone. Lexicographers are now busily un-teasing the strands of Finnish, Modern Greek, Danish, Russian, Czech and Triestine Italian and setting them out neatly. Soon, to anyone with the time and the space for the *Wake* dictionaries, all the linguistic problems of that book will be solved. And the dream itself, being at last lexically intelligible, may seem in danger of dissolving. But the real riddles of the book derive from its subjective, autobiographical quality, the private world of so many of the referents.

The fundamental strength of Joyce's language lies not in its eagerness to expand the lexis – grudgingly, despite everything, most of his readers would admit that this is healthier than a Newspeak contraction of it – but in its loving acceptance of the native idiom. If Milton created a Babylonish dialect, closer to Latin than to Anglo-Saxon, and Hopkins exaggerated the Teutonic matrix of English, Joyce never moved far – except for contrast-pointing dramatic effects – from the rhythms of his native Dublin. Both *Ulysses* and *Finnegans Wake* end up as glori-fications of the linguistic resources of that town, just as the novels of Dickens exalt the resources of nineteenth-century London English. The linguist may approach Joyce through Anglo-Irish as it was under 'the fifth of George and the seventh of Edward' (Stephen being prophetic in Nighttown) and through a battery of foreign lexicons; all the rest is literature.

Bibliography

🐚🐚🐚🐚🐚🐚

There are many books on Joyce – biographical, critical, very few specifically linguistic – and the number increases every year, especially in America. The following are a few that I have found stimulating or informative or both.

BIOGRAPHICAL

Anderson, Chester G., *James Joyce and His World*. New York: The Viking Press, 1967.

Budgen, Frank, *James Joyce and the Making of 'Ulysses'*. Bloomington, Ind.: University of Indiana Press, 1960.

Ellmann, Richard, *James Joyce*. London and New York: Oxford University Press, 1959.

Joyce, Stanislaus, *My Brother's Keeper*. New York: The Viking Press, 1958.

Sullivan, Kevin, *Joyce Among the Jesuits*. New York: Columbia University Press, 1958.

GENERAL–A. BOOKS

Burgess, Anthony, *Here Comes Everybody*. London: Faber and Faber, 1965; (as *Re Joyce*) New York: W. W. Norton, 1965.

Goldberg, S. L., *James Joyce*. New York: Grove Press, 1963.

Gross, John, *James Joyce*. (Modern Masters series). New York: Viking Press, 1970.

Kenner, Hugh, *Dublin's Joyce*. Bloomington, Ind.: University of Indiana Press, 1966.

Tindall, William York, *James Joyce: His Way of Interpreting the Modern World*. New York: Charles Scribner's Sons, 1950.

——, *A Reader's Guide to James Joyce*. New York: Farrar, Straus and Giroux, 1969.

GENERAL–B. ESSAYS IN BOOKS

Daiches, David, *The Novel and the Modern World*. Chicago: University of Chicago Press, 1960.

Stewart, J. I. M., *Eight Modern Writers*. London and New York: Oxford University Press, 1963.

Wilson, Edmund, *Axel's Castle*. New York: Charles Scribner's Sons, 1931.

INDIVIDUAL WORKS

Early Books:

Connolly, Thomas, ed., *Joyce's 'Portrait': Criticisms and Critiques*. London: Peter Owen, 1964. New York: Appleton-Century-Crofts, 1962.

Hart, Clive, ed., *James Joyce's Dubliners: Critical Essays*. London, Faber and Faber, 1969.

Ryf, Robert S., *A New Approach to Joyce*. Los Angeles: University of California Press, 1964.

Ulysses:

Ellman, Richard, *Ulysses on the Liffey*. London: Faber and Faber, 1972.

Gilbert, Stuart, *James Joyce's Ulysses*. New York: Knopf, 1952.

Goldberg, S. L., *The Classical Temper*. New York: Barnes and Noble, 1961.

Mason, James, *James Joyce: Ulysses*. London: Edward Arnold, 1972 (though rather ill-written).

Finnegans Wake:

Atherton, J. R., *The Books at the Wake*. New York: The Viking Press, 1960.

Benstock, Bernard, *Joyce-Again's Wake*. Seattle: University of Washington Press, 1965.

Campbell, Joseph, and Robinson, Henry Morton, *A Skeleton Key to Finnegans Wake*. New York: The Viking Press, 1947.

Dalton, Jack, and Hart, Clive, edd., *Twelve and a Tilly*. Evanston: Northwestern University Press, 1966.

Glasheen, Adaline, *A Second Census of Finnegans Wake*. Evanston: Northwestern University Press, 1963.

Hart, Clive, *Structure and Motif in Finnegans Wake*. London: Faber and Faber, 1962.

Litz, A. Walton, *The Art of James Joyce*, New York: Oxford University Press, 1961.

Tindall, William York, *A Reader's Guide to Finnegans Wake*. New York: Farrar, Straus and Giroux, 1969.

Various Hands, *Our Exagmination round his Factification for Incamination of Work in Progress*. New York: New Directions, 1962.

Wilson, Edmund, essay in *The Wound and the Bow*. London: Oxford University Press, 1947.

Anthony Burgess, in *A Shorter Finnegans Wake* (London: Faber and Faber, 1966; New York: The Viking Press, 1966), provides a lengthy introduction to a version of the work cut down to 251 pages, with explanatory interludes.

Index

꧁꧁꧁꧁꧁꧁

Word-forms and book-titles appear in italics